The New Leader

The New Leader

Harnessing the Power of Creativity to Promote Change

Renee Kosiarek, JD

BEP BUSINESS EXPERT PRESS

The New Leader: Harnessing the Power of Creativity to Promote Change
Copyright © Business Expert Press, LLC, 2016

First published in 2016 by
Business Expert Press, LLC
222 East 46th Street, New York, NY 10017
www.businessexpertpress.com

ISBN-13: 978-1-63157-278-4 (paperback)
ISBN-13: 978-1-63157-279-1 (e-book)

Business Expert Press Human Resource Management and Organizational Behavior Collection

Collection ISSN: 1946-5637 (print)
Collection ISSN: 1946-5645 (electronic)

Cover and interior design by S4Carlisle Publishing Services Private Ltd., Chennai, India

First edition: 2016

10 9 8 7 6 5 4 3 2 1

Printed in the United States of America.

Abstract

Leaders in the 21st-century must learn to solve problems and motivate followers with a combination of creativity, leadership, and effective change. In *The New Leader: Harnessing the Power of Creativity to Promote Change*, readers will develop an understanding of the relationship between creativity, leadership, and change. They will analyze the creative process, learn how to develop a creative culture, and understand effective leadership styles that promote creativity and change. They will explore training to enhance creativity and leadership, and develop practical ways to create an environment that encourages positive growth.

The book offers simple techniques to enhance creativity and leadership immediately, while also pointing to long-term changes that will bring even more success. Stories, reflection questions, and theories are intertwined to help the reader develop sound strategies to lead with enhanced creativity. The book helps an overwhelmed leader learn engaging tools to lead change, while encouraging disengaged leaders to try new methods to revive their leadership and accomplish a motivating vision. In the end, leaders will become more effective, engaging, and transformational by adopting the ideas in the book. They will serve as a model for creativity, create spaces that enhance creative growth, and encourage cultures where employees are free to create positive changes for their organizations.

Keywords

change, creative, creative process, creativity, culture, illumination, leader, leadership, transformational leader

Contents

Acknowledgments

This book would not have been possible without the support of my family. Thank you to my husband, Mike Kosiarek, for your never-ending encouragement and for helping me struggle through these chapters. You challenge me with such insight, but support me every step of the way. I am so grateful for you.

Maya Kosiarek, thank you for showing me what kindness, heart, and imagination look like. Ryan Kosiarek, thank you for showing me how to be creative in so many diverse ways. You both are my heart and my joy and have taught me to see the world with fresh, beautiful eyes.

Thank you to the hardworking people who have motivated me through the years, including my beloved father Robert Krawitz and my friend Connie Ostrowski. Rachel and Dave, you have shown me strength and love in so many ways. Joan Krawitz, thank you for believing in me, reading my drafts, and loving me unconditionally. Deidre Donnellan, thank you for being my rock and my truth teller. Elaine Pietsch and Elizabeth Falzone, thank you for walking this journey with me. And to my Krawitz and Bernstein family: You show me how beautiful family can be. I am blessed to have you all in my life. My family and friends are my greatest blessing, so thank you for supporting and loving me.

I would like to thank Business Expert Press for making this book possible and Andi Cumbo for assisting with the editing process. Thanks as well to all of the teachers and professors who have inspired me through the years.

Finally, I offer sincere and humble thanks to the Leadership, Ethics & Values Program and the Masters in Leadership Studies Program at North Central College, as well as the School for New Learning at DePaul University. I have been able to teach and learn from hundreds of students in these programs and adore working as a professor. Each of my students demonstrates unique strengths that I admire in so many ways. It is a true privilege to work as a professor of creativity, leadership, ethics and change.

Renee Kosiarek, JD.

CHAPTER 1

Creativity

The Crucial Ingredient for Success

Our single greatest asset is the innovation and the ingenuity and creativity of the American people. It is essential to our prosperity and it will only become more so in this century.
—President Obama, March 11, 2010

Status quo, you know, is Latin for "the mess we're in."
—Ronald Reagan

The manager accepts the status quo; the leader challenges it.
—Warren Bennis

So much has changed in the last 20 years.

- **We have become an interconnected world, networked in ways we did not anticipate**. Customers, leaders, and employees live and work all over the world.
- **We have access to data and information on nearly every subject**. This gives clients a chance to easily find solutions to common problems online. It also makes it easier for clients to find your competition and assess their strengths compared with yours.
- **Sometimes, three generations of employees work side by side**. This presents a host of different challenges and rewards, but certainly can make leadership more complex.

- **Employees are now on call 24 hours a day, 7 days a week**.
  Clients, bosses, and peers expect immediate responses to
  problems via email, text, and phone calls. And employees are
  burned out and disengaged.
- **People are expected to communicate in new and unique
  ways**. We want organizations to be able to share information
  in 140 characters or less. But they also must create compelling
  stories discussing their purpose and successes in order to stand
  out and beat the competition.
- **Marketing and sales are more complicated**. Social media,
  LinkedIn, face-to-face networking and affiliations bring
  success in new ways.
- **Services are being phased out as technology advances.**
  Automated tools and vast access to cheap freelance work make
  it easier for clients to do things that were once hired out for
  larger dollars. Companies must continue to develop creative
  service offerings in order to stay ahead.

Unfortunately, leadership has not evolved at the pace of everything else.
We are faced with unique problems every day in our workplaces, and yet
we still rely on hierarchical or sometimes situational leadership. We do not
know how to tackle our problems with creativity, and we are burned out
looking for the right answers to move our organizations and teams forward.

All too often, we are trying to lead people on the basis of outmoded
concepts of hierarchical leadership, relying on power and authority to
motivate workers. Leaders and organizations are clinging to the status
quo because it worked in the past. Rather than building on the unique
strengths of their employees, managers push people to produce quick and
dependable work. Some micromanage while others delegate everything.
They parcel out bonuses and expect full engagement. Or they work in a hierarchical, structured way, leaving little room for challenge and creativity.

This type of leadership may have worked in the past, but it will not
guide us into the future. Top down, hierarchical leadership no longer
works. Neither does micromanaging.

Recently, Harvard Medical School surveyed 72 senior leaders and
found nearly all of them reported signs of burnout.[1] Gallup reports that

only 30 percent of employees in the United States and only 13 percent across the globe feel engaged at work. And fewer than 25 percent of white-collar workers feel connected to their organization's mission. When individuals are not fully engaged, organizational performance suffers.[2]

But there is a way out. This involves creativity and the creation of original and useful ideas.

Creativity is about bringing new, novel, and useful ideas, thoughts, processes, and sometimes art and music to life. When leaders embrace creativity, they bring original and useful ideas to their organization. These ideas may enhance followers' motivation and performance, or boost the success of the organization.

Creativity and creative problem solving make us feel alive; they are part of our humanity. We are the only species that is able to be truly creative. We come up with new solutions and use our brains to discover tools, technologies, and ideas that other animals simply cannot imagine. When we produce new ideas, we feel alive.

Creativity, in fact, is often seen as a peak experience and has been associated with strong mental health and stability.[3] Creative people are typically "engaged, motivated and open to the world."[4] And this type of engagement is what we need in order to enhance our organizations and the people within them.

Try It Yourself

Grab a piece of paper and pen. If possible, also find a comb.

For the next 3 minutes, create a list of 30 or more uses for a comb. Imagine the comb as a tool, utensil, and building block.

Have fun, experiment, and enjoy. There are no wrong answers. Do not censor yourself.

When complete, share this exercise and your results with others.

Now, notice how you feel. Is there a shift in your energy and enthusiasm? Do you feel a bit energized and playful? A bit more alive?

If you are like students in my undergraduate classes, you will notice that creativity brings a palpable shift in energy. Don't we want to create that shift more often in our lives and organizations?

Creativity can also create a sense of accomplishment and success. In surveys and testimonials, people overwhelmingly say that they feel a sense of pride when they share what they create. Some even believe that creativity is an essential component to fulfillment and yearn to create new things and bring innovative ideas to life. As noted psychologist Rollo May says, "If you do not express your own original ideas, or listen to your own being, you will have betrayed yourself." Psychologist and author Mihaly Csíkszentmihályi agrees, stating that "perhaps only sex, sports, music, and religious ecstasy . . . provide as profound a sense of being part of an entity greater than ourselves."[5]

Creativity also enhances a person's sense of value and worth according to some studies, including Adobe's 2012[6] study on people's attitudes and beliefs about creativity at work, school, and home. In this study, Adobe surveyed 5,000 adults: 1,000 from the United States, 1,000 from the United Kingdom, 1,000 from Germany, 1,000 from France, and 1,000 from Japan. The findings were dramatic. Over 80 percent of participants felt that being able to create enabled them to make a difference in their lives, and nearly two-thirds of the people surveyed felt that creativity is valuable to society. As well, over 75 percent of those in the United States felt that being able to create enabled them to make a difference in the lives of others. "The ability to create defines who I am as a person," said almost 70 percent of U.S. respondents.

Unfortunately, the vast majority of people believe that they are not making the most of their creativity. In fact, mo*re than 75 percent of people globally believe that they are not living up to their creative potential.*

As well, most people do not describe themselves as creative individuals. In a recent survey of over 5,000 people, only about 50 percent of respondents in the United States described themselves as creative. In France, the numbers were even lower, with only 36 percent of respondents describing themselves as creative. In Japan, only about 19 percent of those surveyed believed they were creative.[7] And yet scholars and creatives agree that "creative confidence will be a necessary mindset for doing business."[8]

Most people know that creativity is an inherent and important value to enhance businesses in the 21st century. In 2010, IBM asked more than 1,500 CEOs questions about leadership and creativity.[9] These 1,500

CEOs consistently reported that creativity is the single most important leadership competency for enterprises facing the complexity of global commerce today.

In the last several years, politicians, educators, and business leaders in the United States have recognized that creativity is an essential component for economic success. Business and graduate schools see creativity as a desirable factor in admission decisions, and even medical schools are changing the way they educate to accommodate the need for creativity more formally.

Innovative organizations enjoy greater market share than do less innovative ones,[10] and some believe that creativity is a greater predictor of success than intelligence.[11] With our rising global problems and the complex challenges that we have before us, creativity is needed now more than ever. Jobs that don't require creativity are beginning to be automated, and positions and leadership require creativity in order to solve complex ambiguous problems that machines cannot solve.

Creative problem solving can help us navigate through difficult problems and motivate our workforce. Millennials and Generation-Z'ers are moving into the workforce. Many of these people are no longer motivated to work solely for a strong income and security. Rather, they have motivations that are distinct and unique. They yearn to collaborate, contribute, and be engaged. Creativity helps these workers feel that their work matters and gives them opportunities to collaborate on new and novel ideas.

Not only does creativity enhance the livelihood, self-esteem, self-confidence, and motivation of many of our workers, but it also helps us solve complex and ambiguous problems like customer relations, effective marketing in the 21st century, or strong teamwork in a global organization. You can use creativity in many ways in an organization including:

- Developing new and original ways to gain customers
- Determining original and useful ways to hire the best and brightest people for the organization despite limited resources
- Creating new and appropriate methods to retain those individuals, despite limited resources

- Designing new and useful ways to display material, create marketing ads, reach out to new generations of customers, determine branding, and use social media effectively
- Learning and applying original ways to make a grumpy customer happier, keep an old client in her organization, or renew a store that seems lackluster compared with the one down the block
- Exploring new and original methods to lead across generations, in order to engage millennials and all generations in useful and meaningful ways
- Experimenting with original ways to appeal to a broad base of customers and clients across regions and generations
- Finding new and useful ways to build and enhance teams
- Celebrating successes within the organization in new and meaningful ways
- Thinking of new and novel approaches to train and develop the workforce. Boring doesn't motivate ... but original trainings can
- Playing with new and useful ways to make an outsider feel like they are welcome within the organization. Out-groups will be minimized because creative leaders will seek new ways to offer inclusion, even if it takes trial, error, and experimentation

The challenges for you, as a 21st-century leader, are vast. So putting creativity at the forefront of your agenda as a leader makes sense. When you do that, you will consistently explore new, novel, and useful ways to approach the breadth of your duties. Perhaps most importantly, you will inspire and encourage your followers to be creative, and offer a culture and atmosphere that supports such creativity. Sometimes, you will fail, but the successes will be plentiful and the rewards vast. Followers will feel more energized, alive, and engaged, and you will have a renewed sense of passion and vitality.

Unfortunately, at this moment, leaders are not tapping into the potential of creativity. Less than 20 percent of white-collar workers believe they have time for creative or strategic thinking.[12] The culture in which they work prevents them from feeling free to experiment, play, and make mistakes. The space where they work is stifling, allowing little room for flexibility, collaboration, and divergent thinking. And the training they receive is outdated and focused on models of leadership that, while useful, could be enhanced with additional trainings on creativity and change.

Researchers have found that rigid and bureaucratic organizational structures with excessive hierarchies inhibit creativity. Additionally, creativity is stifled when managers are risk-averse and not receptive to an individual's new ideas. Finally, a lack of dialogue and high conflict are also obstacles to creativity.

Noted creativity researcher Theresa Amabile has identified several inhibitors of creativity including a low-risk attitude, lack of autonomy, inappropriate evaluation systems that don't provide feedback, insufficient resources, time pressure, an emphasis on the status quo, and competition between teams and employees that encourages defensiveness.[13]

In sum, the most common ways leaders kill creativity are through:

- A bureaucratic, top-down, fear-based leadership style
- High-stress, high-pressure deadlines and project goals that don't allow time for new ideas
- A culture that makes failure too risky
- A lack of resources to support creativity and innovation
- Depersonalized working spaces that don't allow for collaboration or imaginative thinking
- Lack of long-term rewards
- Failure to align an individual's work responsibilities with their interests and passions
- Lack of clear purpose in organization

Unfortunately, many of our workforce leaders are killing creativity without even knowing it. They want novel, original ideas but send the wrong messages to their employees. They are trying to encourage creativity and motivation but don't really know how to make that spark happen.

This book will show you the way. It will teach you tools, techniques, and concepts that have been proven to enhance creativity, leadership, and engagement. Unfortunately, there are no quick fixes when it comes to creativity and leadership. It does take a commitment, and requires changes within the leader and the organization.

Thus, the book encourages you, as a leader, to take up creativity as the #1 goal of your leadership. Making creativity the cornerstone of your agenda could change everything, but does take determination and work.

In the pages that follow, we will tie together the principles of creativity, leadership, and change to help you make creativity the cornerstone of your agenda. With hard work, persistence, playfulness, and experimentation, you can become a more effective, engaged, and alive leader who succeeds in bringing out the best yourself and those within your organization.

Reflection Questions

1. When was the last time you were creative at work? How did it feel to be creative?
2. What is your personal philosophy on creativity?
3. How might creativity enhance your organization?
4. How might creativity help you become a better leader?
5. What assumptions are you already making that prevent you from leading and working in novel and creative ways?
6. Is there a better way to run your meetings? What new and novel method could you try at your next meeting? What is stopping you from trying it? (For more ideas, see Chapter 9.)
7. What if your followers felt like they were able to contribute something new and novel in the workplace? How might that enhance their energy and engagement?

Notes

1. Schwartz, Tony, and Christine Porath. "Why You Hate Work." The New York Times. May 31, 2014.
2. "More than 200 studies have now confirmed a direct and powerful relationship between the level of employee engagement and company performance." "The Human Era @ Work." Harvard Business Review and The Energy project, 2014. http://documents.kenyon .edu/humanresources/Whitepaper_Human_Era_at_Work.pdf

3. Sawyer, R. Keith. *Explaining Creativity the Science of Human Innovation*. Oxford: Oxford University Press, 2006. p. 171.

4. Bronson, Po, and Ashley Merryman. "The Creativity Crisis." Newsweek. July 10, 2010.

5. Csíkszentmihályi, Mihaly. *Creativity: Flow and the Psychology of Discovery and Invention*. New York, NY: Harper Collins Publishers, 1996. p. 2.

6. Adobe State of Create Study (April 2012). www.adobe.com/aboutadobe/pressroom/pdfs/Adobe_State_of_Create_Global_Benchmark_Study.pdf

7. Ibid.

8. Brown, Tim. "What's Next in the World of Making." IDEO. (Web log). April 3, 2014. http://designthinking.ideo.com/?p=1329

9. IBM Institute for Business Value. Capitalizing on Complexity: Insights from the Global Chief Executive Officer Study." May 2010. www.ibm.com/ capitalizingoncomplexity

10. Some studies have found that innovative organizations have more than 30% greater market share then non-innovative companies. Puccio, Gerald, John Cabra, and Nate Schwagler. "10 Reasons to Flex Your Creative Muscle: From Foursight." World Creativity and Innovation Week April 1521. February 11, 2014. http://wciw.org/2014/02/11/10-reasons-to-flex-your-creative-muscle-from-foursight/

11. Paul Torrance concluded that a child's score on divergent thinking tests were "300% more likely to predict how many inventions, how much creative writing and other creative outputs were produced in adulthood." Thus, divergent thinking appears to be a better predictor of noted creative achievement than does IQ.

12. Schwartz and Porath, "Why You Hate Work."

13. Amabile, Teresa. "How to Kill Creativity." *Harvard Business Review*. 1998.

CHAPTER 2

Finding and Using Creativity in Your Organization

We all know that Picasso, Beethoven, da Vinci, Galileo, Einstein, and Ford were highly creative individuals. Each one created new and novel work that was respected by their communities. But what do we mean when we say they were "creative?"

These individuals produced work that was not mere novelty. They created something novel **and** valuable. They came from a variety of disciplines including business, science, and art. Many of them worked in collaboration with others, not merely in isolation.

For the purposes of this book, we define creativity as the production of an original and useful idea. Everyone can have these sorts of ideas in their organizations and lives. Coming up with creative ideas and sharing them with others will bring life and engagement to an organization.

Creativity Defined Through the Years

Definitions for creativity can vary widely depending on the industry, culture, and person. Some view creativity as lofty, out-of-the-box, esoteric thinking that results in new, often crazy and wild ideas. Others view it as a trait that belongs to the insane.

In the past, the Greeks felt that external forces inspired creativity; humans were not working alone in creating something new. The Western concept of creativity seemed to agree with that premise initially, as it essentially began with the Biblical story of creation as shared in Genesis.

Only in the last several hundred years did the public attribute creativity to something other than a superhuman force.

The Renaissance brought changes not only in artistic work but also in people's understandings about creativity. People began to see artists as unique beings who worked separate from God and the church. These beings, and not necessarily superhuman forces or muses, were responsible for creative works.

The term *genius* was first used to describe creative people in the 18th century. The word *creativity* was not invented until the late 19th century[1] and did not appear in English dictionaries until after World War II.

Leading mathematicians and scientists, such as Hermann von Helmholtz and Henri Poincaré, began to reflect on and publicly discuss their creative processes in the late 19th centuries. Modern creativity research did not really begin, however, until 1950 when noted psychologist Joy Paul Guilford addressed this idea in a presidential speech before the American Psychological Association. During this address, Guilford urged psychologists to explore creativity, stating that "the neglect of this subject by psychologists is appalling." He then went on to emphasize the significance of creativity for business, science, arts, and education and called for more research into the nature of creativity.[2] His pleas worked, as creativity research blossomed after this speech.

We know today that creativity can take several forms.[3] New ideas or concepts, like the invention of the automobile or film, may result from creativity. Creativity also occurs when people modify existing concepts, like turning a play into a film or adding words to an instrumental piece of music. Finally, individuals are being creative when they combine previously unrelated ideas, like the invention of the iPhone.

Creativity is not the finding of a thing, but the making of something out of it after it is found.

—James Russell Lowell

Essentially, creativity can occur by making something entirely new, modifying existing ideas, or combining previously unrelated ideas. How does it work? Consider the examples in Chart 2.1.

Chart 2.1 Creativity Explained

New creations/ideas	Combining existing ideas/creations	Modifying existing ideas/creations
Invention of the **car**	**Go Cycle**—an electronic bicycle	**Recompute**—Computer made out of recycled cardboard
Invention of **film**	**Storage by the Box**—Ship your items via FedEx to a storage facility	**Xeros**—Washing machine that uses 90% less water, relying on nylon polymer to remove stains rather than water
Impressionistic **painting**	**TriSpecs**—Sunglasses with headphones and headset inside	**Fresh Healthy Vending Machines**—replacing candy and chips with healthy foods in vending
Rock & Roll music	**Healthy Snack Subscription**—Monthly boxes of healthy snacks delivered automatically to your door like magazines	Phone conference calls become **videoconferencing**
First **Dry Cleaning** Service	**Gourmet Food Truck**—Gourmet meals served out of a food truck	

The above examples illustrate the power of creating new concepts and ideas. But they also show that creativity can be highly valuable when people combine existing ideas to make something new. As illustrated by the examples above, some very successful businesses have been thriving because of that type of creativity.

Modifying current ideas and concepts also serve companies well and can be used to improve functions, service offerings, and products. For example, we can modify existing products to make them more economical, environmentally friendly, or effective. We can also modify existing ideas about leadership to make it more inclusive, valuable, and effective.

Try It Yourself

Leading creativity researchers believe that we can expand our own creativity when we regularly think differently about problems. Let's practice combining two unrelated ideas to create an original and potentially useful new product or service. Think broadly about options, enjoy the playfulness of this exercise, and do not censor your ideas. Work quickly…

- Grab a paper and pen.
- Make a list of five ways you could combine an umbrella and a pot. Consider how that new invention could be original and useful.
- Next, make a list of 10 ways you can combine a shovel and a television. Perhaps the new inventions will make the product more useful, interesting, or unique, or perhaps you might take apart pieces of the products to make something altogether new.
- Finally, select two people who work in unrelated departments in your office. Brainstorm a list of ways the two could work together to create something new or exciting at work.

"Creativity is just connecting things." It involves an ability to "connect experiences they've had and synthesize new things."

—Steve Jobs

The sociocultural model of creativity was introduced in 1983 by social psychologist Teresa Amabile and provides a slightly different view of creativity. Amabile (1983) stated that "a product or response is creative to the extent that appropriate observers independently agree it is creative." She then went on to define appropriate observers as those who are "familiar with the domain in which the product was created or the response articulated."[4] Here, Amabile was asserting that creativity must be socially approved, as determined by people within a field who confirm the novelty of the work. She says, "I define creativity as appropriate novelty that is recognized as such by people knowledgeable in a domain."[5]

Novelist Henry Miller also believes that creativity must involve a component of value stating, "Creativity is the occurrence of a composition which is both new and valuable." CEO and entrepreneur John Haefele agrees stating, "Creativity is the ability to make new combinations of social worth."[6]

Creativity may happen through a small shift in behavior, or a radical change or discovery. Certainly, there is a component of problem solving in creativity. A leading scholar on organizational creativity Michael Mumford, states that creativity in an organization is "the production of high quality, original and elegant solutions to problems."[7]

Companies often discuss creativity interchangeably with the term *innovation*. Yet, most scholars believe that innovation is not the same as creativity. Creativity, that is, the production of something original, useful, and appropriate, is needed in order to develop an innovative product.[8] Innovation, on the other hand, is not merely a new and useful idea. Rather, innovation is largely about the successful invention or execution of a new product or service often by an entire organization.[9]

Necessity may be the mother of invention, it's true, but its father is creativity and knowledge is the midwife.

—Jonathan Schattke

This book focuses on creativity rather than innovation. Here, we're interested in the original and useful ways you can create change, motivation, engagement, and effectiveness in your organization.

The Characteristics of a Creative Person

In order to become a more creative leader, it is important to understand some of the characteristics of a creative person. That way, you can work to inhabit some of these characteristics into your own life and work.

Truly creative individuals have generally achieved some level of mastery in their work. They have experience, education, and knowledge about their current field that allows them to experiment and develop new and original ways of thinking and working. Thus, a brand new manager, with little experience and education, may find it difficult to be creative on a regular basis at work. She may be too concerned with how to manage the day-to-day affairs of the company and simply lack the ability to think about valuable, out-of-the-box ways to enhance the organization. Similarly, a person brand new to music may be able to play something adequate, but probably will not be able to create an original masterpiece initially. Some level of expertise and experience usually precedes valuable creative outcomes.

Having experience and expertise helps creative leaders understand the current culture of their organization and gives them a sense of the followers' personalities. As an experienced leader, they also know the business structure, strengths, and weaknesses.

> *Creative thinking—in terms of idea creativity—is not a mystical talent. It is a skill that can be practiced and nurtured.*
>
> —Edward de Bono

If someone has mastery and expertise, they can begin to develop creative options. Having some of the characteristics of a creative person will enable a leader to develop creative options with greater ease. In general, creative individuals are confident, independent, passionate, and open to new experiences.

In *Creativity: The Psychology of Discovery and Innovation*, noted researcher Mihalyi Csíkszentmihályi describes 10 paradoxical traits that he found were apparent in highly creative individuals.

1. **Creative individuals often have a great deal of physical energy but also spend time quiet and at rest.** Energy is under their control, and they are not ruled by external circumstances.

    Gustav Mahler is a great example of this. He spent two weeks working tirelessly on the completion of his seventh symphony. Failing to make progress, he traveled to Dolomites, hoping to rest. On the way home, while rowing a boat, inspiration struck and he was able to move forward with the piece. "This sounds like magic—like he had won the musical lottery—but had he not previously spent time and energy trying, unsuccessfully, to write the symphony, it is unlikely that inspiration would have struck."[10] It was, indeed, the energy and rest that contributed to the success of Mahler's 7th Symphony.

2. **Creative individuals tend to be smart and yet naïve at the same time**. So while creative individuals typically have a great deal of expertise and intelligence, they also question things consistently and realize that their knowledge is limited.

   Alex Kipman is the creator behind Microsoft's Kinect motion controller for the X-Box, which became the fastest selling consumer device of all time when it was launched at the end of 2010. He has been listed as one of the top 100 creative people in business by *Fast Company* magazine and has received dozens of awards for his creativity. Yet Kipman works to not only be smart, but also a bit naïve. When he created Kinect, he said he "had to get wicked, wicked smart people to assume stupidity from day one." These people needed to be naïve and smart, so they could explore concepts with a fresh eye and use their expertise to deliver solutions.

3. **Creative individuals are extraordinarily disciplined**. They're responsible but also playful.

   If you are reading this book, you are probably a disciplined leader; you approach work with vigor and determination. As a creative leader, it is also important to be playful. We spend a good deal of time talking about playfulness in this book and include ways to become more playful in Chapters 5, 7, and 9.

4. **Creative individuals can be deeply rooted in reality, but at the same time they have an active imagination**.

   John Reed from Citibank felt that it was important to have a sense of reality but to also know that reality is constantly shifting. He says, "I think we can look at [reality] in so many different ways. Right now in my business, banks are deemed to be successful based on capital ratios. Ten years ago, there was no concept of capital ratio."[11] By being rooted in reality and imagination at the same time, Reed was able to look at his organization in new light and be aware of the limitations of its current view of reality.

   Tony Fadell, creator of the iPod and smart thermostat Nest, also recognizes the value of imagination. He says that designers have to resist habituation and ask themselves questions about the status quo using a beginner's mind. For instance, when looking at ordinary items, Tony often takes a "pregnant pause" to imagine new possibilities. When looking at a toothbrush, he may ask himself if it is made of the best material for bristles or if it is the right-sized handle. In this way, he has a sense of reality but also uses his active imagination to create reinventions that could enhance reality. This practice of beginner's mind allows him to explore original and useful ways to design new products and solutions.[12]

Try It Yourself

Most leaders are rooted in reality. They have to deal with deadlines, employee and client concerns, and other pressures in the workplace on a daily basis. Often, they have little time for imagination. In order to expand this characteristic, let's try having a beginner's mind, even for a couple of minutes.

- Grab your toothbrush, paper, and a pen or pencil.
- Look at your toothbrush and imagine that you are seeing this device for the first time. What could you use it for?
- Then, consider how you might redesign a toothbrush. Pretend that your boss has told you that you MUST recreate it. What would you change, and why?
- Finally, look at a follower in your organization with a beginner's mind. Who is she? What motivates her and lights up her passions? Ignore what she currently "does" in the office, and investigate who she is with a beginner's mind. Consider how you might use this "new" person in the best way possible in your office.

5. **Creative people are sometimes extroverted and other times introverted**.[13] Indeed, creative individuals often find that they get their energy from solitude when working alone or taking a walk

privately. On the other hand, collaboration, which we will discuss in a Chapter 6, is an important part of a creative person's process. So creative people are also extroverted at times, seeking ideas, input, and energy from others, and doing so in a confident and sometimes domineering manner.

6. **Creative individuals are proud**. They're not afraid to share their ideas with others. At the same time, they have a certain sense of **humility**. They're willing to realize that their ideas may be flawed or altogether wrong.

7. **Creative individuals often have components of dominance and submission**. Csíkszentmihályi relates that to psychological androgyny, which refers to "a person's ability to be at the same time aggressive and nurturing, sensitive and rigid, dominant and submissive, regardless of gender."[14]

8. **Creative individuals are independent and rebellious but also somewhat conservative**. They know that in order to be rebellious, they need to have a coalition that will eventually support them in the rebellion. Thus, they can, at times, be traditionalist and conservative.

    Noted choreographer Bill Jones believes a creative individual should not be afraid to be defiant. "Art is made when something is being pushed against. And I think that's OK. That's noble, as a matter of fact. We do not have to be obnoxious with it. We do not have to shut ourselves off in kind of gated communities … But don't be afraid to transgress and say no, and to say you might think this is beautiful, but take a look at this. This is almost the job of a good artist."[15]

9. **Creative individuals are extraordinarily passionate about their work**. They feel deeply connected and have a great deal of energy attached to their work. **At the same time, they are objective**. They realize that all work is flawed, and are willing to take criticism and feedback in a way that may sometimes cause them to completely revamp their work.

    Saul Griffith, a 2007 MacArthur fellow, exudes passion in his work. He created HowToons with the hope of educating children about science and engineering in engaging ways, and also cofounded thinkcycle.com, a website that produces socially conscious engineering solutions. Saul believes passion is paramount to creativity, stating "I don't believe anyone can do anything that they are not passionate about." When hiring people, Saul works to ensure they select projects that fuel the individual's personal passions as well.[16]

Passion is one great force that unleashes creativity, because if you're passionate about something, then you're more willing to take risks.
                                                                —Yo Yo Ma

10. Creative individuals are open and sensitive. **They feel a great deal of suffering and pain as well as enjoyment.** They have a depth to their emotion that may be unlike others.

    Musician Anthony Kiedis feels pain and enjoyment at deep levels. He says, "By experiencing life to its fullest—the extreme spectrum, emotionally speaking—that's what gives me creative impetus. That's what gives me feeling on the inside, just awareness of the world really."[17]

These 10 paradoxical traits are broad:

1. Passionate and objective
2. Energy and rest
3. Proud and humble
4. Introverted and extroverted
5. Conservative and rebellious
6. Dominant and submissive
7. Disciplined and playful
8. Reality-based and imaginative
9. Smart and naïve
10. Feels pain and pleasure deeply

They shape an interesting picture of the creative individual and show characteristics that could be extremely coveted in a strong, creative leader. Chart 2.2 demonstrates this more fully.

Chart 2.2 *Paradoxical Traits of Creative Individuals*

Paradoxical traits	Example for how those traits could be helpful
Passionate and objective	He fiercely shares the mission of the organization and works to ensure its success, but remains open to discussing new possibilities for the organization as well.
Energy and rest	She approaches work with zest and energy, but also takes time for vacations, weekends with family, and holidays. She sets an example for employees to do the same.
Proud and humble	He shares his work product freely and with pride, but remains open to making it better through engaged feedback and dialogue with superiors and subordinates.
Introverted and extroverted	She works well alone and takes time to meaningfully reflect. She also is energized when working collaboratively with groups on projects.
Conservative and rebellious	He is cautious not to present ideas that are completely out of the box without context. Yet, he breaks the mold regularly and does share original ideas that may seem rebellious, but always are supported by contextual reasons for the rebellion.
Disciplined and playful	She works hard and puts in long hours to ensure the success of her employees. At the same time, she has a great sense of humor and can lighten the mood during a difficult day.
Reality-based and imaginative	He respects each person's role within the organization, but also imagines new possibilities for engaging employees. By regularly engaging them in small projects that are vastly different from their current obligations, he offers employees new challenges and opportunities for growth.
Smart and naïve	She knows her stuff and is widely seen as the expert. She also knows that, despite being the "expert," she has a lot to learn and regularly reads and listens to others in order to gain new insights and knowledge.
Feels pain and pleasure deeply	He senses the joy and pride of his subordinates when they gain a new client and celebrates fully with them. He also feels loss deeply and knows the toll that sorrow can have on a person's work. He brings this knowledge with him to work and honors the varying emotions of life.

We know that it's important for leaders to have a great deal of expertise. But sometimes this expertise may lead them in the wrong direction. As a leader, it is important to be open to feedback and criticism even when you have expertise.

A leader will, of course, be disciplined and hard working. Yet we also want one who is playful—who can celebrate successes, encourage risk taking, and try new things. That playfulness and discipline can ensure that work gets done, but do so in a culture where people can make mistakes, take risks, and even enjoy the workplace.

Being rooted in reality is deeply important for leadership. As a leader, you need to understand your clients' needs, demands, and experiences. Yet at the same time, reality is consistently changing, and your clients' needs will as well. When you are most effective, you will be able to forecast your clients' future needs by imagining possibilities for the future, and exploring new and useful ways of serving your clients and employees.

You will also have lively collaboration meetings and joint sessions with your followers to ensure the success of your organization. At the same time, you will take time to reflect in solitude and carefully consider all options before moving forward on important initiatives.

While reflecting, humility is often in order. As a strong leader, you will consider your own shortcomings and own up to your mistakes. At the same time, you will show a strong sense of pride not only in your organization but also in your organization's projects and employees.

You will have a level of emotional intelligence and be able to feel the joy and sorrow of life deeply. This helps you have empathy for others and is one of the reasons you are respected by your employees. They know that you are a person of great emotional depth and wisdom, and others appreciate your vulnerability and compassion. Your employees know that you are passionate about your work, as you share that passion regularly. At the same time, you remain objective and do realize that there may be new ways of doing things that you had not anticipated. This passion and objectivity help you see and develop creative ways to maneuver through the next century.

In totality, these paradoxical traits of creatives are incredibly useful for strong leadership. But interestingly, many other traits of creatives can also be useful for leadership in general, and particularly for creative leadership.

Other Traits of Creative Individuals

Dr. Gary A. Davis, psychologist and author of several books on creativity, says, "As an R&D manager, your job is to get the most from the people with creative potential. That's never simple, but the more you know about the abilities and personality traits of creative people, the easier it will be."[18] In his research, Dr. Davis found that creative individuals are:

- Thorough
- Ethical
- Emotional
- High energy
- Curious
- Open minded
- Humorous
- Risk taking
- Fantastical
- Artistic
- Perceptive
- Original
- Independent
- Attracted to complexity and ambiguity
- Energized by alone time
- Aware of their own creativity

Attraction to complexity and ambiguity are traits that are commonly seen in creative individuals since original, unique, and useful ideas often are ambiguous; We don't know for sure if they will work because they're new. However, the messiness of complexity and ambiguity can be challenging for many leaders. In fact, people like to have the answers and certainty is a coveted quality for many individuals.

Creative leaders, however, need to be tolerant of that ambiguity and somewhat attracted to complexity. They know that there are many different ways to motivate followers or get customers to their organizations. They recognize and appreciate the complexity of this and work to develop new and useful ideas to meet the needs of employees and customers.

Finally, most creative individuals are open to new experiences and ideas. They like to explore new ways of doing things and are rather flexible in general. Creative individuals like to break free from routine, experiment, and try new things. They are alert and observe the world around them carefully. Strong leaders should do the same.

The Creative Process

It is important to develop the characteristics of creatives, such as being open to experience. But it is equally important to become comfortable with the creative process. For knowing how to navigate through the creative process will help you become more comfortable in your work.

Most researchers believe that there are essentially four stages in the creative process: preparation, incubation, illumination, and verification.

Preparation

Creativity typically involves some sort of discovery process or preparation. The preparation stage is usually the first step in a creative process; however, people often return to stages of preparation throughout the process.

Many creative individuals work tirelessly to gather the right tools, books, and materials before beginning work. They conduct research on a topic and gather all of the required background information before trying to come up with a creative solution. They may reformulate the problem, seek new ways to frame the problem, and gather the appropriate tools before ever trying to develop a creative new product, offering, or idea. That sort of preparation is part of the creative process.

However, people prepare in different ways. Some begin brainstorming creative options without much background information at all, and others require a good deal of research and preparation before going further. Either way can work, depending on the individual. Indeed, there is no one right way to prepare.

For instance, many writers research their settings and characters before writing their stories. They may visit the city explored in their book and take copious notes on its appearance, culture, and vibe. They may observe the people within that city, taking note of attire, demeanor, and characteristics before ever developing a single character for the novel. But some writers do not prepare in that sort of depth. Poet Parker Palmer says, "For me, writing does not begin with reaching for expertise by gathering facts, wrapping them in lucid thoughts, then downloading all of that from my mind to the page. It begins with making a deep dive into something that baffles me—into my not-knowing—and dwelling in the dark long enough that 'the eye begins to see' what's down there. I want to make my own discoveries, think my own thoughts, and feel my own feelings before I explore what conventional wisdom says about the subject. That's why I'm not so much a writer as a rewriter, most of whose scribbling goes through eight or ten drafts."[19]

In the end, it is important to know that preparation is part of the process, but that it looks different to different people. Sometimes, preparation means merely getting your paper and pen. Other times, it involves hundreds of hours of research, investigation, and questioning. Then, the preparation process may feel endless. But it is part of the process, and necessary in order to achieve true creative growth.

Incubation

The next stage of the process is often referred to as incubation. This stage is an important component of creativity that may happen after preparation or in any other phase of the creative process. It can happen in any number of ways, but basically occurs when you step away from your creative problem and do not consciously think about it. Perhaps you turn your attention to another work matter. Or maybe you take a purposeful break from creativity by going for a walk, sleeping, or taking a shower. Sometimes, incubation happens when a person becomes frustrated or overwhelmed with the project and just takes a break or vacation.

Mathematician Henri Poincare was one of the first individuals to write about the creative process and recognized the value of incubation in his writing. He said, "Often when one works at a hard question, nothing good is accomplished at the first attack. Then one takes a rest, longer or shorter, and sits down anew to the work. During the first half hour, as before, nothing is found, and then all of a sudden the decisive idea presents itself to the mind. It might be said that the conscious work has been more fruitful because it has been interrupted and the rest has given back to the mind its force and freshness."[20]

Elon Musk, the CEO o"f SpaceX and chief product officer for Tesla Motors, often comes up with his design ideas while taking a rest from work. Sometimes, his ideas have come while taking a shower, as that may be "his only free time."[21] And designer Sarah Foelske believes that stepping away from your project can be very helpful, stating, "There's usually a time in any project when a stuck moment happens, and I find that getting away from the computer and the busyness of the day is the most important part in successfully battling that. Even if it's only for 10 minutes. When you rest your mind, the ideas will come easier. I find any exercise and meditation really helpful."[22]

Try It Yourself

Take a Break: We are moving in a very fast-paced world. Everybody is multitasking, and demands are immediate. Yet our time and energy are limited during the day. Studies suggest that our mental performance starts to deteriorate after about 50 to 60 minutes of continuous work. We begin to zone out, lose track of time, and start to second-guess ourselves. The good news is that energy can be refilled by rest.

In this try-it-yourself activity, we focus on taking purposeful breaks:

- Spend time at lunch at least once a week doing something completely distinct from work and your creative problems.
- Step away from your work when you notice heightened levels of frustration. Rather than push through to completion, try taking a break. Let your unconscious mind try to solve the problem while your conscious mind steps away from it.
- After having worked on any project for two hours, turn to something new, even if for a short time.
- Take a couple of days every so often to completely unplug from your creative problem. Try not to think about it at all. Sometimes, magic happens when you step away from the problem.

Illumination

Illumination, the third stage of creativity, occurs when you have that "aha" moment of discovery or insight. It happens when the creative person has an idea that does indeed seem novel, unique, and useful.

Lawrence Bragg, winner of the 1915 Nobel Prize in Physics, had almost given up hope of finding an answer when, while walking, "the whole thing came clearly in front of him" in a flash. This burst of illumination occurred during a period of incubation, but only after he was already a master of physics.[23]

Brian Eno, composer and musician for U2 and Talking Heads, also speaks of the power of illumination, stating, "You're just treading water for quite a long time. Nothing really dramatic seems to be happening. … And then suddenly everything seems to lock together in a different way. It's like a crystallization point where you can't detect any single element having changed. There's a proverb that says that the fruit takes a long time to ripen, but it falls suddenly … And that seems to be the process."[24]

This sudden insight is exhilarating. It is often the moment that people yearn for when working on their projects. But it should be noted that the creative process does not end with illumination. Typically, some sort of verification is needed in order to ensure that the creative work is original and valuable.

Verification

Verification is the process of collaborating with others to determine whether the new idea is indeed useful and original given the circumstances. During this verification stage, you will confirm or invalidate the work. This process might lead to success and completion of your work, or may lead to frustration and further incubation. Perhaps, at this point, you may return to the preparation phase and reframe the problem. Or maybe you will decide you no longer want to work on the problem. At some point, you may suddenly have a new, useful, and appropriate idea for how to tackle that very same problem. You might refine that idea a bit and then verify it again with others.

As you can see, the four stages of creativity don't necessarily go in any order. Rather, they occur somewhat randomly with preparation often being the first step and a step that individuals return to again and again as they refine their thinking on various problems.

Many people believe that the creative process is only about those light-bulb "aha" moments. And while some people certainly do have flashes of inspiration, creative thinking and new and useful ideas usually come about through hard work, dedication, intelligence, and knowledge of the field. You see, it's very difficult to adequately prepare and reframe a problem if you're not even sure what the context of that problem is. So the original, useful ideas will most often come from conscious thinking, work, play, experimentation, and reframing of problems. They arise oftentimes not because you are struck with a divine moment of clarity but rather because you have many years of expertise and knowledge in your field that allows you to combine ideas in original and useful ways.

Filmmaker John Cleese exemplifies hard work, play, experimentation, and incubation phases in his often creative process. He attributes his own success largely to the fact that he gives himself uninterrupted time to think, play, and complete his work. For instance, he sets aside a certain number of hours a day, usually about two hours, to work on creating and developing new ideas. During this time, he locks himself in a room and devotes himself solely to the task at hand, creating new and useful work. He might have an "aha" moment within the first hour, where he thinks he has suddenly created the best, brightest, and funniest skit. But he doesn't end his period of work there. Rather, he gives himself the full two hours to continue to develop these ideas, even when he thinks he might have already discovered the best one. Often, this means he will simply be "wasting time" sitting quietly in his office doing absolutely nothing. And yet, it is those periods of "wasted time" that he believes can create the best, most illuminating works.[25]

Most people find that they are very good at one of the four stages of the creative process. For instance, some people are excellent at framing the problem, gathering their tools, and preparing for how they're going to solve the problem. Others are good at collaborating, verifying, and getting feedback from other people about their creative idea. Some are fine with waiting and not having answers to their creative problem; incubation, to these people, is more than acceptable.

When you are able to work through the creative process fully, you will take their time to create new and useful business models and strategies to propel the organization forward. Perhaps you may use the creative process to develop new ways of serving clients by tweaking previous service models, or maybe you will develop new and useful ways to work with a supplier. But in the end, a leader who cultivates characteristics of creativity and works through all four stages of creativity will be able to develop better, more original, and more useful ideas that propel the organization forward.

Reflection Questions

1. Looking over the list of 10 paradoxical traits, what are your strengths and weaknesses?
2. Choose one set of opposing traits and write why it would be important for you to develop these traits in your organization and leadership.
3. What are three ideas that you can implement now to enhance these traits in yourself?
4. How might you use this list to help your followers be more creative?
5. Which of the four stages of creativity comes easiest to you?
6. Which of the four stages is most difficult for you?
7. Why is each of these stages critical to the creative process?
8. How can you become more comfortable with each of these four stages?
9. Do you allow your followers to practice these four stages of creativity, giving them time to prepare, rest, incubate, and verify ideas?

Notes

1. Sawyer, *Explaining Creativity: The Science of Human Innovation*, 19.
2. Guilford, J. Paul. "Creativity Research: Past, Present & Future." Lecture, The 1950 Presidential Address to the American Psychology Association, January 1, 1950. www.cpsb.com/research/articles/creativity-research/Creativity-Research-Guilford.pdf
3. Creativity researchers often refer to four different definitions of creativity; big-C, little-C, mini-C, and professional-C creativity. Big-C creativity is defined as new, novel, and appropriate creative works that

are recognized by those in the field as such. It relates to clearly recognized and appreciated creative contributions, such as the gates of paradise, the discovery of a new planet, and Beethoven's 9th Symphony. Those works were all new, original, useful, and appropriate contributions to the world that were recognized by experts in the field as such. Little-C creativity is about the production of original and useful ideas and concepts. Different from big-C creativity, little C creativity does not require experts in the field to evaluate and determine that the concepts and ideas are appropriate, novel, and useful. It occurs when an individual writes a new and useful jingle for a commercial or creates an original and useful business model. Mini-C relates to personal individual creativity and is defined as original and personally meaningful interpretation of experience, actions, and events. Here, a child's "aha" moment of discovering that a triangle is the best way to support her building is a mini-C creative moment. To this child, the moment of discovery is new and novel. And while such new and original ideas might not be useful to an adult, it certainly is useful to the individual. Mini-C creativity is measured against the person's own level of development and largely associated with children. Pro-C or professional-C creativity represents developmental and effortful progression beyond little-C. Those who attain professional level expertise in a creative area are likely to have attained this pro-c status. Many amateur artists are creative at the pro-c level, even if it's not their primary means of income. For purposes of this book, we will explore research from big-C, pro-C, and little-C creativity.

4. Amabile, Theresa. "Big C, Little C, Howard, and Me: Approaches to Understanding Creativity." *Harvard Business Review*. 2012.

5. Ibid.

6. Haefele, J.W. Creativity and Innovation. New York, NY: Reinhold Publishing Corp. 1962"

7. Mumford, Michael D., Kimberly Hester, and Issac Robledo. "Methods in Creativity Research." *Handbook of Organizational Creativity*. London, UK: Academic Press. pp. 39–65.

8. Creativity is the core of innovation and is necessary to develop innovative business concepts. Hisrich, Robert D., and Claudine Kerney. *Managing Innovation and Entrepreneurship*, 2014.

9. It should be noted that there does not seem to be a unilaterally accepted definition for innovation. Indeed, researchers vary widely in how they define innovation. Many believe that innovation relates to implementation of creative ideas, usually by a team. For purposes of this book, I am choosing to focus on creativity, defined as the production of a new, original, and useful idea. Of course, the leader will often implement that idea. If we parsed words, some would say that the implementation is then innovative. Practically and for purposes of the text, the terminology makes little difference.

10. Irvine, William B. *Aha!: The Moments of Insight That Shape Our World*. Oxford, UK: Oxford University Press, 2014.

11. Csíkszentmihályi, *Creativity: Flow and the Psychology of Discovery and Invention*.

12. Martin, Courtney. "The Potential in the Pregnant Pause." *On Being*. March 27, 2015.

13. It should be noted that research on introversion/extroversion of creative types produces varying results. Some find that creative individuals are typically introverts, but Csikzmentmihalyi's research found creative individuals have introverted and extroverted characteristics. In particular, creative individuals are often confident, ambitious, and dominant, all traits that are seen in extraverted individuals. However, they do like to work alone, at least some of the time. In a sense, it is important to recognize that a number of creative individuals find energy when working alone, as well as collaboratively. They also share characteristics of introverted (energy gained by working alone) and extroverted individuals (confident and dominant).

14. Csíkszentmihályi, *Creativity: Flow and the Psychology of Discovery and Invention*.

15. Interview with Bill Jones. NPR. May 30, 2013.

16. Hennessy, Leslie A. *Decision Making and Creativity: A Qualitative Study of MacArthur Fellows*. (Doctoral Dissertation). San Diego, CA: University of San Diego, 2014.

17. Boyd, Jenny. *Musicians in Tune: Seventy-five Contemporary Musicians Discuss the Creative Process*. New York, NY: Simon & Schuster, 1992. p. 248.

18. Davis, Gray A. "Article 34—Personalities of Creative People." Article 34—Personalities of Creative People. www.winstonbrill.com/bril001/html/article_index/articles/1-50/article34_body.html

19. Palmer, Parker J. "Three Eternal (So Far) Truths about Living and Writing." *On Being*. April 1, 2015. www.onbeing.org/blog/three-eternal-so-far-truths-about-living-and-writing/7442

20. Poincaré, Henri. *Science and Method*. General Books, 2010.

21. "Elon Musk." Fast Company. May 18, 2011.

22. Blanda, Sean. "10 Creative Rituals You Should Steal." 99u. January 10, 2014.

23. Barron, Frank. *Creators on Creating: Awakening and Cultivating the Imaginative Mind*. New York, NY: Putnam, 1997.

24. McDowell, Scott. "Developing Your Creative Practice: Tips from Brian Eno." 99u. May 29, 2011.

25. Popova, Maria. "John Cleese on the 5 Factors to Make Your Life More Creative." Brain Pickings. April 12, 2012. "John Cleese on Creativity." YouTube. www.youtube.com/watch?v=Qby0ed4aVpo

CHAPTER 3

Strong Leadership

The Foundations

Bad leaders will kill original ideas before they have a chance to hatch. They will discourage growth and be unable to inspire needed change and creativity in an organization. It is, therefore, crucial that organizations employ strong leaders.

So what does it mean to be a leader? There are literally thousands of definitions for leadership.

A number of definitions relate to power and a person's ability to influence others. In fact, most leadership definitions include a component of **influence, inspiration,** or **motivation.**

> John Maxwell states, *"Leadership is about influence; nothing more, nothing less."*
> Peter Drucker says, *"The only definition of a leader is someone who has followers."*

Some definitions discuss the need for a leader to create a shared goal or vision.

Warren Bennis defines leadership as the capacity to translate vision into reality and says "The manager has his eye on the bottom line; the leader has his eye on the horizon."[1]

Noted Professor Peter Northouse states, "Leadership is the process whereby an individual influences another toward the achievement of a common goal."[2]

Gary Yukl takes this idea one step further by requiring leaders to seek consensus on a shared vision. He defines leadership as "the process of influencing others to understand and agree about what needs to be done and how to do it, and the process of facilitating individual and collective efforts to accomplish shared objectives."[3]

The U.S. Army also talks about motivation, stating, "An Army leader is anyone who by virtue of assumed role or assigned responsibility inspires and influences people to accomplish organizational goals. Army leaders motivate people both inside and outside the chain of command to pursue actions, focus thinking, and shape decisions for the greater good of the organization."[4]

Some definitions of leadership talk about change. John Kotter is a professor and researcher on leadership who says, "Leadership defines what the future should look like, aligns people with that vision, and inspires them to make it happen despite the obstacles."[5]

Other definitions talk about community and service. Peter Senge says, "Leadership is the capacity of individuals to spark the capacity of a human community—people living and working together—to bring forth new realities."[6] Servant Leader Robert Greenleaf believes that "leadership is about service to others and a commitment to developing more servants as leaders. It involves co-creation of a commitment to a mission."[7] Gandhi agrees, noting, "Leadership at one time meant muscles. But today it means getting along with people." Finally, former CEO of GE Jack Welch believes that "when you become a leader, success is all about growing others."[8] As John Quincy Adams says, "If your actions inspire others to dream more, learn more, do more and become more, you are a leader."

From this, one thing seems clear: In order to be a strong, 21st-century leader, you must inspire followers to achieve goals and help them grow, develop, and thrive. Only then will your followers feel free to be creative in their approach to work.

Manager Versus Leader

Management is doing things right. Leadership is doing the right things.
—Peter Drucker

It is important to consider the difference between a manager and a leader because leaders who merely manage will not fully inspire their followers or help them thrive in an engaged, creative manner. Management is largely about planning, budgeting, organizing, and staffing, as well as producing predictability and order. Sometimes management can also be about controlling, monitoring, and organizing followers in an organization.

Leadership is different. A leader establishes a direction, develops a vision, and creates strategies to help people achieve that vision. Leaders align the right people, rather than just "organize" them. They motivate, mentor, inspire, and energize people, rather than just control and classify them.

We need more than management to excel as a creative organization. Very few followers will share truly creative (i.e., original and potentially useful) ideas with leaders if they are simply being "controlled" by managers. In order to feel free to share new and useful ideas, followers need to feel mentored, motivated, and inspired by their leaders. Micromanagement will not work.

The new strong leader will work to change the status quo. They plan for the long-term and focus on the purpose of the organization. They communicate and deliver a compelling vision, get people inspired by the vision, and look to the future. A manager does not do this. He works with the status quo, asking "what" rather than "why," and planning for short-term goals.

We need managers to organize individuals, plan for short-term issues, help execute visions, and ask, "What needs to be done?" Budgeting, planning, organizing, and staffing—all of that needs to happen. But true leadership involves much more. And it takes a skilled leader to make it all happen.

Try It Yourself

When our mental models about leadership vary, our effectiveness as leaders may falter. Consider this: A leader with a collaborative approach may be viewed as indecisive and ineffective by a follower who believes that leadership is about influence and authority. However, the collaborative leader may believe he is effective, progressive, and transformative.

(Continued)

Are there varying ideas about what leadership is within your organization? How might those varying mental models affect your ability to lead? Let's find out:

- First, write your own definition for leadership.
- Then, ask five people in your workplace to also define leadership.
- Explore the similarities and differences in those definitions and consider how the opposing mental models may impact how you are perceived as a leader.

Power and Leadership

Power—good or bad, we need it in order to lead. Sometimes we must use our power to encourage followers to take on a challenge and try to be creative. However, power is not the same as leadership. Power is defined as the ability to influence others, and can come in many forms.

Take Bob and Jim, for example. Bob is a vice-president with the power to hire, fire, promote, and advance people. He can use his power to assign interesting work to deserving individuals, or to thwart certain employees. He favors various individuals in the organization and uses his power to punish and reward these people. Most find Bob repugnant: He does little actual work, screams orders at new employees, and manages up. He uses his power for organizational and sometimes personal gain without considering the individual needs and collective culture within the group. Bob has actual power, but lacks leadership skills. Followers don't take chances with Bob: They do as they are told, and little else, for fear of repercussions.

On the other hand, people admire Jim, a middle-manager who oversees a team of five. Jim is not able to directly fire people or assign promotions or bonuses. However, he is highly respected and well liked and can influence leaders at the company with this power of relationships. Sometimes, Jim encourages employees to think outside the box. He often asks them to brainstorm new methods of advertising their work and encourages followers to bring all ideas to the table. When creative ideas are suggested, Jim shares those ideas with upper management and gives the employee credit for such ideas. Because of that, employees know that Jim will use his power to advance not just their ideas, but also their contributions. In this way, employees are motivated to develop and share creative ideas and methods.

Who would you rather work for: Bob or Jim? Most would rather work for Jim.

Bob has power. But his power is based on his position alone and often stifles creativity.

Jim, on the other hand, holds less positional "formal" power, but is able to inspire others because of the power he has developed through relationships. This "informal" power can be highly valuable to a leader.

Karl Albrecht discusses the difference between formal and informal authority in his book, *Social Intelligence; The New Science of Success*, stating,

> Formal authority, obviously, comes with position power—someone or some entity, such as a president or prime minister, a governor, a mayor, a board of directors, or an electorate—has anointed you formally and has granted you a certain range of authority. Earned authority, on the other hand, does not come from others in power positions; you get it from other people, one at a time. You can earn authority by behaving in ways that cause others to consider you worthy of the right to influence them.[9]

Well-liked individuals can and do hold power, often known as *referent power*. People also earn *expert power* on the basis of their skills, knowledge, and competencies, or *reward power* on the basis of the ability to reward followers. Finally, those with authority often use *coercive power* that derives from the capacity to punish others.

In the end, positional, coercive, and reward power can be useful for leaders. But often, more can be accomplished when a leader has power that comes from strong relationships or expertise because followers are intrinsically motivated to help that leader. Thus, leaders should work to grow that type of power.

Try It Yourself

To think and act like a powerful person, people do not need to possess role power or recall being in a powerful role—they just need to arrange their bodies in a powerful way.[10]

In "Power Posing: Brief Nonverbal Displays Affect Neuroendocrine Levels and Risk Tolerance,"[11] Amy Cuddy, Dana Carney, and Andy J. Yap show that simply holding one's body in "high-power" poses for as little as two minutes results in higher levels of testosterone (the hormone linked to power and dominance) and lower levels of cortisol (the "stress" hormone). Holding these power poses leads to increased feelings of power and a greater tolerance for risk. The stances have been shown to help people perform better in interviews and feel more confident overall.

So let's try to hold some power poses ourselves, in an effort to increase our confidence and power.

- **Assume the classic**: Wonder Woman—Keep your feet spread, hands on the hips, and take up space. Hold for two minutes.[12]
- **Sit down and grow powerful**: Assume an expansive position by putting one arm on the armrest of your own chair and the other arm on the back of a nearby chair. Cross your legs so that the ankle of one leg rests on the thigh of the other leg. Stay in that position for two or more minutes.

At the end of these stances, reflect on your feeling of confidence and power.

Then, try the poses every day for a week and work to grow your own sense of power.

Doing so may enhance your confidence and help you become more comfortable with your own power, which is necessary for effective leadership.

Power can be a useful tool to achieve a vision, and leaders of every position can increase their power by building strong relationships within their organizations. Stephen Covey believes in the power of relationships, stating,

> The more a leader is honored, respected and genuinely regarded by others, the more legitimate power he will have with others. Depending on how leaders deal with others (which includes both real and perceived intent, interactive capacity and interactive history), the honor followers extend to them will increase or decrease and the legitimate power in relationship will increase or decrease. To be honorable is to have power.[13]

Unfortunately, leaders are often reluctant to use their power to advance goals.[14] Sometimes, they equate power with control and do not want to be seen as manipulative. Other times, they feel that use of power may actually diminish relationships. But thoughtful use of power is important to maintain and grow relationships and organizations.

Great leaders should use their power to challenge and encourage followers to take risks, try new approaches, and fully engage with work and the organization. Their power can be a nudge that motivates a follower to develop and actually share a creative idea or method. And that new idea or method may be just what the organization needs in order to grow.

Leadership Theories

It does take more than power to lead. Over the years, leadership researchers have actively been trying to decipher what a good leader looks like, acts like, and behaves like.

The great man theory is one of the first theories of leadership and is important to consider because of its historical significance. Under great man theory, researchers claimed that leaders were born, not made, and emphasized that a person could not develop leadership potential. Leaders were strong, confident, and assertive. To the researchers, these traits were innate from birth.

Over time, the great man theory has largely been rebuked, with research showing that leadership can be developed through experience, education, reflection, and mentoring. In the last 65 years though, numerous studies have explored the common traits among leaders. Across industries and generations, intelligence was found to be significantly correlated with leadership. As well, leaders typically had a high level of self-confidence, integrity, determination, and sociability.

Most of our well-known leaders are confident, intelligent, and determined. Mother Theresa possessed a quiet, inner confidence while Martin Luther King, Jr.'s confidence roared in his energizing speeches. Nelson Mandela's determination is evident, but different from Steve Job's. And while both Gandhi and Walt Disney were intelligent, their intelligence was expressed in very different ways.

Sociability also looks different depending on the leader. Sociability relates to a person's ability to work with others. For leadership purposes, sociable individuals maintain positive relationships by being courteous, empathetic, friendly, and cooperative. Abraham Lincoln was able to be sociable with his "team of rivals," and Jack Welch, former CEO of General Electric, did the same through his workouts. In these workouts, employees of GE at all levels were given platforms to share concerns, ideas, and conflicts related to work. Welch and other leaders at GE listened to the employees with empathy and concern and worked to build cooperative solutions to problems. In this way, Welch demonstrated strong people skills, as well as sociability.

Trait Theory of Leadership

Researchers have discovered several common traits in leaders, as shown in the image to your left. Words in bold have been associated with leaders, in a number of studies, across years and generations

Across the globe, certain leadership traits are universally associated with positive leadership, as discovered in the GLOBE study. The GLOBE study was a collaborative, multicountry study of what constitutes good leadership across the world. Over 17,000 individuals from 65 countries participated in this study.

Across all 61 countries in the GLOBE leadership study, people want their leaders to be trustworthy, just, honest, decisive, and so forth. However, how these traits are expressed and enacted may still noticeably differ from society to society. For example, for a leader to be described as decisive in the U.S., he or she is expected to make quick and approximate decisions. In contrast, in France or Germany, being decisive tends to mean a more deliberate and precise approach to decision-making.[15]

The GLOBE study found that leaders are also commonly encouraging, dependable, positive, dynamic, motivational, intelligent, communicative, excellence oriented, and motivational.

Many of the traits associated with strong leadership are also found in creative individuals, as evidenced by Chart 3.1.

Chart 3.1. Traits of Leaders and Creative Individuals

Traits of leaders (mostly U.S. research)	Traits of successful global leaders	Traits of creative individuals
Intelligent	Intelligent and informed	Mastery—creative individuals typically need to have some mastery/intelligence, at least in their given domain[16]
Sociable/extraverted	Team builder	Extraverted and introverted— Creative individuals are a mix of both, as discussed in Chapter 2
Motivated	Excellence/performance oriented and motivational	Passionate
Confident	Confidence builder (Note that confidence does not appear as a trait of global leaders universally.)	Confident[17]
Determination	Dependable and excellence oriented	Determination

While trait theory of leadership wasn't aimed at helping people cultivate new traits, it does provide guidance about the common traits we find in leaders and can be useful in that regard. If you know, for example, that you lack confidence, then it is probably prudent to develop this trait based on the theory. Similarly, if you lack determination, it might be worth analyzing how you could improve this trait in order to become a more effective leader.

Skill Theory

Skill theory of leadership can also be instructive, as it highlights the common skills of highly effective leaders and explores how to develop those skills. Robert Katz pioneered this work, establishing a three-skill approach that can be useful to help you understand the different types of skills that are needed in order to be a successful leader. According to Katz, leaders need technical, human, and conceptual skills to varying degrees, depending on their level of leadership. When you have strong knowledge and proficiency in a specific type of work or activity, you have technical skill. If you are equipped with human skills, you cooperate, have empathy, use conflict-resolution skills, and show courtesy; essentially, you can work well with other people. Conceptual skills relate to big-picture thinking and the ability to work with broad ideas and concepts. If you are able to draft a compelling and inspiring vision or strategic plan, you show conceptual skills.

When you are at the lower level of leadership, you need a significant amount of technical skills. You are carrying out many of the day-to-day tasks and must know how to execute on those tasks. Like all leaders, you also need high levels of human skills in order to collaborate and work well with others. However, at the lower level of leadership, you need very little conceptual skills: you are not the one setting the vision and thinking about long-term goals and objectives.

When working in middle management, you still need high levels of technical skills because you are completing the work and regularly in the trenches. Similarly, you need human skills to work together collaboratively and peacefully with others. As a midlevel leader, you are starting to think about long-term goals and objectives, and now need a higher level of conceptual skill. At this level, you are not only fulfilling a vision, you are creating and implementing new visions and learning how to inspire different types of people. To do this, you need to have high levels of conceptual skill.

Like midlevel leaders, those in the "C" suite or at the top level in an organization will, assuredly, need to have strong conceptual and human skills. However, you don't need the same level of technical skill because most of your time is spent on the big-picture needs of the organization. You are planning, envisioning, and strategizing in a way that provides little time to actually complete the technical work.

In all, the skills you need to succeed as a leader vary depending on your level in an organization. If you are at the top level of leadership, you need stronger conceptual and problem-solving skills, which demand creativity and flexible thinking.

Try It Yourself

In "A Whole New Mind: Why Right Brainers Will Rule the Future,"[18] Daniel H. Pink argues that current global conditions are setting the stage for a brand new era: the "Conceptual Age." In this age, right-brain skills and creativity will be key, calling for us to go beyond just knowledge or expertise. "The best employees of the future will excel at creative problem solving and different ways of thinking—synthesizing seemingly diverse things together for better solutions, using metaphors to explain new ideas for which no context yet might exist."[19]

Let's use our conceptual skills and imagination to create a metaphor that can be used to represent one of your organizational goals or objectives. Using your right brain in this purposeful way will begin to "train" you to think differently about problems and may, in time, help enhance your conceptual skills.

- Develop a goal that you have for your organization or the world. Try to create a goal that is somewhat original to your work, but could be useful. You do not need to share this goal with anyone, so take a risk in drafting the goal and make it a bit unique.
- Without censoring yourself, make a list of 3 to 5 metaphors that could be used to describe the goal. For instance, you could describe the goal as a circle of peace and collaboration, or a money garden. Have fun with this list, and be sure to include one corny, even bad metaphor, just for fun.

Emotional Intelligence

Many of us have all been brought down by leaders who bring their "bad moods" to the office. Likewise, we dislike it when a leader overglorifies the positives at work and fails to consider or have empathy for employees' struggles. Emotionally intelligent leaders understand the impact their mood has on others and manage their emotions so as to provide the greatest good. As well, they have strong levels of empathy, self-awareness, and regulation skills. They don't "dump" their bad days on others, but also don't paint rainbows where followers feel clouds.

This sort of intelligence, known as emotional intelligence or EQ, is a necessary trait for effective leadership and may be more important than general intelligence. Emotional intelligence allows us to understand both ourselves and our followers. People with high levels of emotional intelligence are able to cope with the pressures, demands, and needs in their personal and professional lives.

Emotional intelligence is a needed trait for 21st-century leaders who want to inspire creativity. When you have high EQ as a leader, employees feel understood and appreciated at a deep level. They can authentically be themselves and may be more willing to try new approaches at work. As well, since you create a respectful and safe culture, employees may share creative ideas and concepts more readily.

Daniel Goleman is the leading researcher on emotional intelligence. He writes that there are five different components of emotional intelligence.[20]

- Leaders need to be self-aware and understand their own moods, emotions, motivations, and drives.
- Emotionally intelligent leaders should control their moods, emotions, and impulses appropriately. They are vulnerable and open, but not in an oppressive or overwhelming way.
- Those with EQ have motivation and passion to pursue their goals with energy, zest, and vitality. They are fully engaged, and their followers know it.
- Those with emotional intelligence possess a great deal of empathy. They are aware of their followers' feelings, are able

to put themselves in other people's shoes, and understand the complex emotions and motivations of followers.

- Finally, emotionally intelligent individuals have a great deal of social-skill proficiency. They are able to manage and even mitigate conflict, and work with different types of teams and followers effectively.

Emotional intelligence makes sense. Followers want to see their leader's emotions, believe they have high levels of self-awareness, and feel assured that their leaders can regulate emotions so as not to "blow up" at inappropriate times. It is no surprise then that companies are investing in EQ training.

Google is one such company. Marc Lesser, known as Google's Jolly Good Fellow, is tasked with "enlightening minds and opening hearts." He teaches a two-day course called "Search Inside Yourself" to an estimated 1,500 Googlers. People are clamoring to take the class and become more self-aware, as thousands of individuals wait for future open seats to attend the "Search Inside Yourself" course. Lesser uses the five components of emotional intelligence as the foundation for his training and finds that focusing on EQ helps leaders become better listeners and think more calmly and clearly. He says "emotional-intelligence skills support collaboration, more open communication, more transparency and less posturing, less ego, and more people working for the greater good and for the purpose of the organization succeeding."[21]

Since most leaders want enhanced collaboration and open communication, you should work to enhance your own emotional intelligence.

Try It Yourself

Everyone can work to enhance their EQ. Choose one of the four components of EQ listed below, and pay attention to this area for the day or week.

- Self-awareness: How are you feeling today? What are your emotions? What is motivating to you today? How are you expressing your emotions?

(Continued)

- Self-regulation: How are you expressing yourself today? Do you think before you speak? Are you sharing too much, or withholding too little? Could you be more open, transparent, and vulnerable, showing your followers more of yourself? Or should you hold back a bit? How might a small shift enhance your leadership?

- Motivation and passion: How passionate are you about your goals? Rate yourself on a scale of 1 to 10. If your score is less than 7, consider why you are working on that goal. Try to heighten your level of motivation and passion by thinking about your role in the work, and how the work contributes to a larger purpose. Every follower recognizes a leader without passion. And it is very hard to be passionate as a follower if the leader is not fully engaged and energized by the work. So, grow your passion, or delegate or dump the task.

- Empathy: Take some time to think about one of your followers today; consider her emotions, needs, and motivations. Put yourself in her shoes, and imagine why she comes to work, what sustains her, and what brings her joy. How does she feel in her office, with her workload, etc.? Continue to think about her throughout the day.

Emotional intelligence is directly related to the success of creative initiatives and leaders. Four in 10 people cannot work together cooperatively, and more than 50 percent of employees lack the motivation to keep learning, improving, and creating. As an emotionally intelligent leader, you will work to understand what motivates individual followers and be skilled at helping groups work together. You will also be flexible in your approaches, bending to the needs of your followers. Situational leadership theory can help you understand when to be flexible and shift your behavior, and provides some strategies for how to make those shifts.

Situational Leadership and Other Theories

Situational leadership theory was developed by Hersey and Blanchard in 1969. The theory helps leaders understand the importance of being flexible and teaches them how to change their behavior depending on the follower's needs.

In essence, the theory tells leaders that they should be either:

- Directive: Giving clear instructions and guidance about how to accomplish a task or goal
- Coaching: Providing instructions about how to accomplish a task, but also motivation and support throughout the process
- Supportive: Providing motivation and support to followers
- Delegating: Giving followers autonomy and freedom to complete the work on their own, without direction or consistent support

In the film *Remember the Titans*, Coach Boone presents himself as a flexible, situational leader. The film is about the integration of two suburban schools' football teams in Virginia. Early on, the integration was difficult. Players were not aligned. They did not know how to form a team or train for success. Coach Boone was extremely directive at this stage, telling them how to dress, talk, and train. He said, "You drop a pass, you run a mile. You miss a block, you run a mile."

When the players finally understood how to train and work as a team, Boone moved to a more supportive style of leadership. He felt the players had worked hard and were a bit deflated. He offered them support and motivation, making them run to Gettysburg. At Gettysburg, he gave them an inspiring speech, stating "55,000 men died right here, fighting the same fight we are still fighting ourselves." "Take a lesson from the dead," Boone said. "If we don't come together, right now on this hollow ground, we too will be destroyed just like they were."

Boone's leadership was unparalleled because he changed his style to suit the followers' needs. Near the end of the film, he delegates a task to a student captain, trusting this individual to make a decision for the team about another player. In this calculated delegation, Boone empowered the follower, and led well. Yet, by offering direction and motivation at other times, he also led well. The trick was that he was flexible in a calculated way. He essentially used situational leadership principles to succeed.

Situational leadership may also enhance creativity. Again and again, research demonstrates that people need to tinker, experiment, and fail in order to produce original and useful work (see Chapter 6). Essentially then, creativity demands flexibility and resiliency. A situational approach helps a leader enhance creativity in the organization by showing them how to be flexible in a somewhat calculated, yet proven, way.

So, if you want to enhance motivation and creativity, it is important to be flexible in the right way, at the right time. To do that using situational leadership theory, you first assess the follower. Are they competent and skilled to complete the task? Are they motivated?

Then, you assess the situation.

- If your follower is excited and motivated about the task but lacks knowledge about how to accomplish it, you should be directive. Here, your follower needs direction because this particular task is new, he/she is new to the organization, or he/she lacks experience with the task.
- If your follower lacks motivation about the task and lacks skill, then you should use the coaching approach. This approach requires direction and support.
- If your follower lacks motivation but knows how to complete the task, then you should support them: you could remind the follower of the purpose of the work, or just take them to lunch to show appreciation. Do not give them overwhelming direction. If you direct a follower in this circumstance, you will be demotivating and could be seen as a micromanager.
- If your follower with task knowledge is also motivated, then you should delegate the project. Even offering high levels of support can be demotivating to the highly motivated, experienced follower. This follower wants to be trusted with work, and delegating the task enables them to thrive.

Putting the Theories to Work

Not long ago, people thought leadership could not be developed. Leaders had innate personality traits like intelligence and sociability that could not be enhanced.

Now, we know that leadership can be enhanced and developed. We can become more open, sociable, flexible leaders. We can grow our emotional intelligence and become more empathetic. And we can hone our skills to become a more proficient conceptual thinker.

Unfortunately, you can still falter as a leader even with strong traits, emotional intelligence, and flexibility. Your followers' needs are immense, and your business is likely complex. Thus, in addition to developing skills, flexibility, and emotional intelligence, you must work to become a transformative leader.

Reflection Questions

1. How would you assess your intelligence, confidence, sociability, determination, and openness to experience? Can you improve some of these traits?
2. How would you assess your human, technical, and conceptual skills? Depending on your role in the organization, do you need to improve your technical or conceptual skills?
3. Looking at the five components of emotional intelligence—self-awareness, self-regulation, motivation, empathy, and social skill—which one is your strength and which is your weakness?
4. How can you enhance your emotional intelligence? Create three goals for this month that may help you enhance your ability to be self-aware or self-regulate, or may grow your motivation, empathy, or social skills.
5. Are you a flexible leader? Do you practice situational leadership?
6. Looking at situational leadership, what is your preferred leadership style? Do you prefer to direct, motivate, or delegate?
7. Think of a time where you should have done the opposite of your preferred leadership style based on your follower's needs. How might you have been a more effective leader had you applied that style of leadership to the situation?
8. How might being flexible and applying various styles of leadership to your followers create greater effectiveness for you as a leader?

Notes

1. Bennis, Warren G. *Managing the Dream: Reflections on Leadership and Change*. Cambridge, UK: Perseus Publisher, 2000.

2. Northouse, Peter G. *Leadership: Theory and Practice*. 5th ed. Thousand Oaks, CA: Sage Publications, 2010.

3. Yukl, Gary A. *Leadership in Organizations*. Englewood Cliffs, NJ: Prentice-Hall.

4. Department of the Army. "Army Leadership." http://armypubs.army.mil/doctrine/DR_pubs/dr_a/pdf/adp6_22.pdf

5. Kotter, John P. *Leading Change*. Boston, MA: Harvard Business School Press, 1996.

6. Senge, Peter. "Leadership in a Living Organization." *Leading beyond the Walls*. San Francisco, CA: Jossey-Bass, 1999.

7. UNC Executive Development. "Can You Define Leadership?" September 22, 2015. http://execdev.kenan-flagler.unc.edu/blog/can-you-define-leadership

8. Lowe, J. (2007). *Jack Welch Speaks: Wit and Wisdom from the World's Greatest Business Leader.*

9. Albrecht, Karl. *Social Intelligence the New Science of Success*. San Francisco, CA: Jossey-Bass, A Wiley Imprint, 2006.

10. Paul Murphy, Annie. "How Powerful People Think." Time Magazine. April 22, 2013.

11. Carney, Dana R., Amy J. C. Cuddy, and Andy J. Yap. "Power Posing: Brief Nonverbal Displays Affect Neuroendocrine Levels and Risk Tolerance." *Psychological Science,* 21, no. 10: 1363–1368. 2010.

12. Buchanan, Leigh. "Leadership Advice: Strike a Pose." Inc.com.

13. Covey, Stephen R. *Principle-centered Leadership*. New York: Simon & Schuster, 1992.

14. Since the bible, leaders have been reluctant to use power. Brooks, David. "The Reluctant Leader." New York Times. September 11, 2014.

15. "Culture and Leader Effectiveness: The GLOBE Study."

16. Many researchers believe that there is no correlation between creativity and intelligence if the threshold IQ is over 120. Others believe that creativity and intelligence are not related at all. That said, variables like openness to experience are highly related to intelligence and creativity. Kaufman, James C. *The Cambridge Handbook of Creativity*. Cambridge, UK: Cambridge University Press, 2010.

17. Most researchers agree that mastery of a domain is needed in order to be creative in a useful and meaningful way. Csikszentmihalyi, *Creativity: Flow and the Psychology of Discovery and Invention*; Sawyer, *Explaining Creativity the Science of Human Innovation*.

18. Pink, Daniel H. *A Whole New Mind: Why Right-brainers Will Rule the Future*. New York, NY: Riverhead Books, 2006.

19. Bodell, Lisa. "Work Skills You'll Need to Survive the 'conceptual Age' - CNN.com." CNN. July 17, 2012. www.cnn.com/2012/07/17/opinion/work-skills-future-conceptual-bodell/

20. Daniel Goleman. (1998). What makes a leader? *Harvard Business Review*. pp. 93–102

21. Giang, Vivian. "Inside Google's Insanely Popular Emotional-Intelligence Course." Fast Company. March 25, 2015.

CHAPTER 4

The Transformational, Creative Leader

Some people lead in a directive fashion and believe in top-down, hierarchical methods of managing people. Others build strong relationships with groups of followers and lead those groups using the power of relationships as a guide. Some leaders are charismatic, and some are rather introverted and demure. In the end, directive, supportive, charismatic, and demure leadership can all work to enhance effectiveness and creativity. But transformative leaders combine these attributes and behaviors at the right time and are able to bring out the best in their followers. They are strong role models who motivate and challenge their followers on an individual basis.

In order to be transformative, you must be a strong role model. You simply will not be able to encourage and engage followers if you are seen as a "fake" or "fraud." Yes, you need to possess the traits and skills we discussed in Chapter 3, including conceptual skills, high human skills, strong emotional intelligence, and empathy. But those skills and traits will not work if you do not model yourself as someone who is creative at work.

A leader leads by example, whether he intends to or not.
—John Quincy Adams

As a transformative role model, you may seek out original and useful ways of looking at information and engaging with the world. Perhaps you experiment and try new activities. Maybe you explore new books, music, dance, or even sports. You then share your outside experiences and perspectives with those in your organization, being transparent about your creative mistakes and successes. In this way, you show your followers that curiosity and experimentation are welcome, as are mistakes and failures.

Jeff Bezos, the founder and CEO of Amazon.com, presents himself as a role model for creativity. He is determined, hardworking, and extraordinarily passionate about his work. He also has a barrage of interests that span well beyond Amazon. He is an inventor himself, having developed a 10,000 year clock. He founded Blue Origin, a space company aimed at bringing everyone into space. He also patented an airbag system for cellphones and invented a solar cooker as a child. Bezos believes that invention and experimentation are crucial at Amazon, and encourages employees to be inventors and "explorers." He serves as a role model in terms of exploration and creativity. His behavior sends a message to employees, telling them that they should engage with the world in diverse ways and try new things.

Try It Yourself

Begin, right now, to explore the world in new and original ways.

- Read a section of the newspaper you have never read, pick up a new genre next time you are at the library, or listen to a type of music you have never explored. Consider why these stories (or music) appeal to people, and think about how they could perhaps be relevant to you.
- What kind of person do you know nothing about? The Humans of New York project captures images and quotations from random New York City residents and visitors. Explore the website (www.humansofnewyork.com) and read about people who are different from you. What can you learn from them? What lights them up? What is their perspective on life, and how can that perspective enlighten you?
- If you had to run a meeting differently, how would you do it? Imagine you had to incorporate drawing, silence, or mind-mapping into your meetings. How could you do that? Why not try it?

Are you placing enough interesting, freakish, long shot, weirdo bets?
—Tom Peters

So how does one become a role model in terms of creativity? First, as seen by Bezos, you must experiment, play, and try new things. As well, you could work on cultivating the characteristics of creative individuals that were discussed in Chapter 2. And finally, you could build habits that enhance creativity.

Habits and Behaviors to Enhance Creativity

Robert Grudin, a leading creativity researcher and author, believes that creativity is a habit that can be cultivated throughout life. He says, "Habits might be called an ethos of inspiration—not a birthright, but a demanding and integral code." In this way, a transformative leader who is a role model will work to cultivate some of Grudin's creative habits including the following:

- **Love of the problematic:** "To be open to inspiration, one must cultivate a leaning for the problematic, a chronic attraction to things that do not totally fit, agree, or make sense."[1]

  As a creative leader, it is important to grow your love of the problematic. Consider how you might be able to view conflict differently. When an employee, with a "reasonable" workload, seems upset because he claims he is overworked, can you shift your perspective and look at the problem with fresh eyes? What might be causing his feeling of overwhelm? Might it be a lack of passion for the particular project, issues with child care, or failure to give him enough positive feedback? Or is your definition of reasonable workload off? Might you, in fact, be underresourced as a company? As a lover of the problematic, you will explore the issue deeply and look for thoughtful solutions to solve the problem.
- **Boldness:** "To be attentive to new messages, to sift them for validity and mercilessly reject the invalid, and to follow good

ideas in spite of their forbidding strangeness all take a kind of courage"[2] and boldness.

Are you bold and courageous enough to share unusual ideas with others? If you don't model that, how can you expect that from your followers? As a transformative role model, it is crucial to adopt a habit of courage and boldness. Look for new, original, and even odd ideas. Share those that seem worthwhile proudly, even when the concept may be rejected as unrealistic or bold. If you don't share your bold ideas, who will?

- **Courtesy:** "Great innovators address their own studies with appreciation, deference, and even humility; they excel in activities, like the revision or destruction of their own inferior work."[3]

  How do you react when given feedback and criticism? Are you willing to critique your work? Are you open to addressing your flaws? As a creative role model, it is important to critique your work thoughtfully and accept criticism with grace. You must be willing to destroy work that is not serving your organization, even if that work took weeks. Developing courtesy as a habit and choosing humility and deference over ego will serve you well.

- **Openness:** Inventive people transcend alternatives, rethink problems, and generate new alternatives. They look at the world with open eyes and wonder.

  Can you be more open-minded? Are you able to explore issues from multiple angles, or do you just consider one point of view? As a creative role model, it is important to transcend the obvious on a regular basis so that it becomes a habit. Seek to look at the world with a beginner's mind, as discussed in Chapter **2**.

- **Consequence:** "To be consequent is to view every success as a step in an ongoing venture, every failure as a substantial discovery in a mission of trial and error."[4]

  Do you accept failure, or do you dislike it and try to avoid it at all costs? To be a creative role model, it is important to view successes **and** failures as part of your mission. You must build a habit of accepting failure on a regular basis, rather than shunning it. You must share this habit with colleagues and communicate that failures are an acceptable part of the creative person's journey.

- **A passion for work, playfulness, and love of beauty:** Creative work "is self-expression, self-fulfillment. As such, it is a pleasure that ranks with sport and love and laughter and all the other better things in life. In the creative life, leisure is not a contrary of work, but rather a compliment to it."[5]

  Do you have a passion for your work? Does it align with a bigger purpose in your life, beyond the finances?

Some of these habits are difficult to master. Passion for work, in particular, is simply absent for many of us. We work for the money and security, and seek joy elsewhere. And while that may be acceptable, it will not be transformative.

If you want to be a transformative leader, you must work to grow your passion for work. People in almost any industry can do that. Nick Sarillo provides an excellent example for consideration. He owns a pizza restaurant in the suburbs of Chicago. The kitchen is hot, and sometimes the restaurant is understaffed. But Nick has a passion for work. He yearns to create a restaurant that makes customers feel like celebrities. He believes in his employees, and passionately works to empower them to be their best selves mentally, physically, and emotionally. He teaches the employees listening skills that help them at work and in life. He is passionate about being of service to others, and models passion for work and life. Nick encourages creativity at work by giving employees freedom to develop new marketing methods and events. As well, he himself is creative because he has chosen to run his pizza place differently. It is not about the pizza; rather, it is about the experience for both the customers and the employees. And this creativity works. "Nick's Pizza & Pub has margins nearly twice that of the average pizza restaurant … and boasts an 80 percent employee retention rate in an industry in which the average annual turnover is nearly 150 percent."[6]

Like Nick, you can work to grow your passion for work. If you don't feel connected to the product or service you are offering, ask yourself how that service/product may help others. Perhaps you can grow your passion by thinking about the impact your work has on customers or employees. Might your service or product make people's lives easier or more joyful? And how does your work serve employees? Perhaps you continue to employ numerous people, providing them with food, shelter, and maybe even education for their families. Often, we ignore those outcomes and feel that our work is meaningless. When you reflect on them, you may find your passion for work expand.

You may also expand your passion for work by exploring the "beauty" in life, as Robert Grudin calls it. Grudin says that "a healthy sense of beauty is one of the key factors in the passion for work that dissolves the work–leisure dichotomy."[7] Essentially then, a creative individual will look for the beauty in work and life on a consistent basis. For instance,

- If you pay attention to the "beauty" in your employees, you will be far more likely to take the time to understand the employees' strengths and put those strengths to work. That will inspire the employees and help them be more engaged: a win-win for all.
- If you pay attention to the beauty of an existing product, you may see new potential uses for that product.
- If you pay attention to the beauty of order, you may create new organizational systems that enhance the overall effectiveness of your organization.

In addition to a love of beauty, creative individuals possess a habit of playfulness. Playfulness allows the leader to experiment and accept original and useful ideas. Russ Johnson, author of *Play: The New Leadership Secret that Changes Everything*,[8] encourages leaders to play regularly. He proposes leaders incorporate humor into trainings, form a fun committee, and host friendly competitions between departments in the office. He suggests that playfulness begins with the leader, and will enhance effectiveness, creativity, and engagement in an organization.

> *More than 75% of respondents in a survey done by the Society for Human Resource Management believe that companies that promote fun at work are more effective than those that do not.*[9]

As the leader, you must model playfulness and cultivate that as a habit. Let yourself play, paint, create music, try a new joke, and experiment with new ideas. Look at a product and think about how you can make it different. Play with how to change your space and yourself.

Try It Yourself

Let's be a little playful. Take out a blank piece of paper and a pen or, better yet, markers or crayons if that's available. You are going to draw a picture of yourself. No one will see it.

- Imagine you are a super hero. Your power: You are an amazing, transformative role model. What characteristics do you have? How are you dressed? Are you enormous? Do you have a cape? Can you fly?
- Now, draw a picture of yourself as the superhero. Make some big muscles on the picture and write words around it that describe your super hero powers.
- Have fun, experiment, and PLAY! Don't censor yourself.
- Feel free to use metaphors and analogies . . . and mostly, enjoy!

Your employees are looking to you as their leader. If you are not engaged with life and looking for original and useful ways to expand your business, grow your followers, and just live life, then what kind of message are you sending to your followers? How can you expect them to come up with original and useful ways to engage with life, create ideas, and energize those around them if you don't model that? They look to you as the example. Being creative and sharing your new and potentially useful ideas is risky because the idea may be so new, that it's just unworkable. But, if you aren't putting forth your original ideas and facing rejection, then neither will they.

So be a role model. Put forth your original and useful ideas. Work to develop habits of playfulness, passion for work, openness, love of the problematic, and courtesy. Show your followers that you fail and sometimes succeed. And in so doing, you will teach them what creativity looks like, and give them permission to cultivate these useful habits as well.

Inspiring Motivation

Imagine motivated, engaged, and creative followers. They enjoy being at work, get more done, and contribute in meaningful ways to the organization. They know their purpose in the organization and use their strengths to excel. They have a passion for work and contribute to a culture of engagement and positivity.

Transformative leaders help inspire that kind of passion and motivation in their followers. They share a vision that resonates deeply, and are able to help followers see purpose behind their work. It is not an easy job to inspire motivation in followers, but it is possible.

As a leader, you need to think about four key components to inspire motivation in followers. First, you must give individual consideration to each follower. Then, you must challenge them. Third, you need to reward your followers and give them feedback in appropriate ways so as to enhance motivation. And finally, you must create a vision and values for the organization that resonate with employees. Let's explore each of these in turn.

Individual Consideration to each Follower

> *What leaders have to remember is that somewhere under the somnolent surface is the creature that builds civilizations, the dreamer of dreams, the risk taker. And remembering that, the leader must reach down to the springs that never dry up, the ever-fresh springs of the human spirit.*
>
> —John W. Gardner

Each of our followers has unique strengths, weaknesses, interests, and passions. Situational leadership helps us understand when to direct, support, or delegate. But, situational leadership is only a starting point. As a transformative leader, we need to give direct, focused, and individual attention to each follower. We must tap into our followers' unique personality in order to see what makes them tick. This begins with curiosity and exploration. We should consider exploring these questions:

- How is the follower creative?
- What makes the follower feel "alive?
- What is the best project the follower ever worked on, and why?
- What is the follower passionate about in general, and at work?
- What does the follower want others to say about him/her?
- How does the follower want to be remembered?
- What does the follower yearn to do and learn?

As a leader, we must use our human skills to be this type of explorer. We need to engage with each of our followers, and listen deeply to their passions, interests, and desires.

Too often, we, as leaders, are working to grow the weaknesses of our followers. And while that sometimes needs to be done, transformative leaders will pinpoint the unique strengths in each of our followers and give them some opportunity to work from those strengths. A person working from strengths will excel far faster than one working from weakness. They will also create more success for the organization. Transformative leaders know this, and help followers use strengths as a springboard to success by changing their language, focus, and sometimes direction.

To help your followers work from strengths, you might consider small shifts, as referenced in Chart 4.1.

Chart 4.1 Using Strengths: A Guide

From this ...	To this ...
Focusing solely on the followers' weaknesses	Focusing on the follower's strengths and looking to find more ways to use those strengths in the workplace
Forcing the follower to trudge through work that seems impossible to him	Reassigning the task by looking for someone else to complete the work who might find it easier and more natural (i.e., someone whose strength lies in completing that sort of task)
Letting the follower feel defeated for her shortcomings	Pointing out the follower's strengths and working with her to put those strengths to work
Listing the things the follower did not do well	Recognizing the tasks the follower does well while also noting those that need work

This sort of individual consideration takes time, effort, and positivity. But it can be extremely rewarding for the follower and leader.

It takes more than looking at strengths to succeed. As a truly transformative leader, you should also individually consider how your follower is already creative. Is he a painter or a photographer? Does she like to problem solve and brainstorm, or solve crossword puzzles? Does she like to find original ways to lead teams or mentor others? Did he like to build with Legos as a child, or make huge forts at home? Was she once a musician?

After exploring how each and every follower is individually creative, transformative leaders will try to bring some component of that creativity into the workforce. How might that work? It varies.

- As a transformative leader, you may discover that one of your employees loves decorating rooms and planning parties. You could then encourage him to plan the holiday party. This way, he has something that he loves to do in the workforce, at least on occasion.
- Another follower may be a musician. In this instance, you should speak to the follower about her interest and offer opportunities to help on her musical path. Perhaps you could ask her to design a team-building event around music during lunch, or encourage her to create the playlist for the holiday party. You might even give her time off to take music lessons during the day.

In this way, a transformative leader uses job crafting to help followers bring creativity to work. A job is "a collection of tasks and interpersonal relationships assigned to one person in an organization. Job-crafting theory elaborates on classic job design theory that focuses on top-down process of managers designing jobs for their employees."[10] In job crafting, employees use opportunities to customize their jobs and tasks.[11]

Job crafters may take on more or less tasks, expand or decrease the scope of their tasks, or change how they perform their tasks altogether. An accountant who enjoys creating organizational systems might create a new method of filing taxes. A person who enjoys art may ask to assist in developing marketing pieces for the organization. And one who likes to write could be the "storyteller" at the firm: the person who shares client and employee stories that enhance motivation in weekly meetings or email blasts.

Sometimes job crafters may simply alter how they perceive their tasks. For instance, a person who thinks of herself as a cook might change her perception, calling herself "an artist who serves beautiful, healthful life to customers." An insurance agent may reframe his work and see it as a way to help people get back on track after a health crisis. And a trainer may begin to see her work as an opportunity to help others live and work with more pride, dignity, and confidence. Finally, a custodian could reframe his work and see that he is the gatekeeper of beauty and cleanliness in the building.

Southwest Airlines' flight attendants reframe their roles in this way. They regularly sing, tell jokes, and take care of customers with creativity. Jill Simonson, regional leader of community affairs and grassroots for Southwest, has said our people "see each flight as a new audience that they can entertain: They do an amazing job of creating a fun and entertaining experience 35,000 feet up."[12]

Travelzoo's employees also reframe their roles. They are not merely customer service agents looking to book the next deal. Rather, their work serves a higher purpose. "To hear managers describe their work in meetings, however, booking a customer on a cheap trip to the Caribbean can serve a higher purpose: helping someone get over the death of a loved one or meet a future spouse."[13]

Transformative leaders will work to craft and reframe tasks in this way so that work becomes more meaningful to each individual follower. Doing so will allow these followers to be more engaged, creative, and inspired.

Try It Yourself

Let's reframe the way we look at some tasks in your organization.

- Make a list of your job requirements.
- Try to reframe these tasks so that they inspire some motivation in you. For example, instead of organizing files, you could reframe your work as "providing cleanliness, order, and ease in the office."
- Next, do job crafting with a follower in your organization. Sit down and talk to her about some of her current job duties. Make a list of the tasks and then reframe some of these jobs in a way that may make the tasks more personally motivating.
- Finally, explore whether, as a transformative leader, you can shift some of the tasks that aren't engaging and/or add tasks that might be interesting and creative so the follower is more passionate at work.

Sometimes, job crafting may be key to enhancing creativity and engagement on an individual basis at work. Other times, it may be important to give your employees some time to pursue their personal interests and creative pursuits. Ricardo Semler, the CEO and majority owner of Semco Partners in Brazil, believes that it is important to do that and finds giving employees time to pursue their passion enhances engagement and effectiveness at work. For that reason, he encourages followers to "take Wednesdays off" to climb mountains, write a book, or become a strong guitar player. And this perspective works: under

Semler's ownership, revenue grew from $4 million in 1982 to $212 million in 2003.[14]

In the end, a transformative leader will enhance engagement by individually considering each employee's needs and interests, particularly with respect to creativity. Job crafting can help put those interests to work. Giving them some outside time to pursue passions may also lead to greater success.

Challenge and Progress

Exploring your followers' individual strengths and using job crafting can bring greater purpose. Still, followers will eventually become disengaged if they are doing the same job day after day without any new challenge. A transformative leader will offer challenges, autonomy, and opportunities for growth that enhance motivation long term. Even in traditional routine jobs, transformative leaders can figure out ways to challenge a follower.

- A follower on an assembly line who has excelled at work may be given opportunities to train or mentor new employees.
- An administrator could be challenged to participate in strategy meetings, even if only occasionally. Collaboration from a variety of perspectives not only challenges the administrator, but, as we will see in Chapter 6, can enhance creativity in an organization.
- An intern at a social service agency could be tasked with doing an informal "assessment" of the strengths and weaknesses of the organization. This task may bring a new, outsider's opinion that challenges that status quo. If framed as an "exercise" to the new employee, such work could be unique, challenging, and motivating as well.

Giving your followers opportunities to grow, be creative, and step out of their comfort zones is crucial to retention and engagement. But challenge is not enough. Transformative leaders must also support followers when they are being challenged.

Leading creativity expert Teresa Amabile says, "Of all the things that can boost emotions, motivation, and perceptions during a workday, the single most important is making progress in meaningful work. And the more frequently people experience that sense of progress, the more likely they are to be creatively productive in the long run. Whether they are trying to solve a major scientific mystery or simply produce a high-quality product or service, everyday progress— even a small win—can make all the difference in how they feel and perform."[15]

Amabile discovered the power of progress in a multiyear research study of creativity. In this study, members of project teams responded to a daily survey for about four months. These projects all involved some component of creativity such as managing product lines or solving complex problems. The daily survey asked participants about their emotions, mood, motivation, and perceptions of the work environment. Amabile and her team carefully looked over 12,000 diary entries and found that people are simply more creative and productive when their inner work lives are positive. "Fully 95% of the managers who took the survey would probably be surprised to learn that supporting progress is the primary way to elevate motivation." In fact, Amabile found that if a person is motivated and happy at the end of the day, "it's a good bet he or she made progress … If the person drags out of the office disengaged and joyless, a setback is most likely to blame."[16]

Don't you feel better when you feel like you've made progress on something?

Amabile found that even ordinary incremental progress can increase people's engagement at work, leading to enhanced creativity. Thus, she encourages individuals to write down one or two events daily that indicate a small win or possible breakthrough.

Challenging followers and tracking their progress will keep them engaged and enhance creativity. Discussing this progress at weekly meetings is prudent, as is tracking and sharing your own progress at work.

Try It Yourself

Let's keep track of our progress this week.

- At the end of each day, make a list of three things that you have done well. Consider your organizational goals as well as your larger purpose in life: Have you ruled out a possible method at work, made a coworker happier at lunch, connected with a friend, or tried something new?
- Share this list with some of your followers. Serve as a role model and talk to them about the research behind the Progress Principle.
- Try to pinpoint a team member or follower's progress at least once every day. At the end of the week, ask yourself if you supported followers by recognizing their contributions and progress.
- Finally, at the end of the week, reflect. Do you think that keeping track of your progress inspired some motivation to continue your work? Did it enhance your creativity in any way? How might it have enhanced your leadership of others?

Vision and Values for the Organization

Transformative leaders inspire motivation in followers by giving them individual consideration and challenge, and by paying attention to their progress. But that still is not enough. Transformative leaders must create values and a vision for the organization that excite and motivate the followers.

Several key factors are important when creating a vision. First, the vision should represent the shared views of most employees in the organization. Thus, as a transformative leader, you should get input on the vision from all stakeholders. You will ask employees questions like:

- What does our organization currently value and why?
- Do we value creativity? Why or why not?
- What is our current vision (see if employees know it), and what is missing in that vision?

- Where do you want this organization to go in the next five years?
- How does our work help others?
- What kind of things could we include in a vision that would energize and motivate you?

When you seek input from others about vision and values in this way, then your employees often feel more connected to the vision. You can then use that input to create a vision for how the organization fulfills a larger purpose in the world. When you seek input from others about vision and values in this way, then your employees often feel more connected to the vision. For instance, Apple's vision inspires followers because it creates a sense of purpose and excellence. It says, "Apple is committed to bringing the best personal computing experience to students, educators, creative professionals, and consumers around the world through its innovative hardware, software, and internet offerings." Facebook's mission "to give people the power to share and make the world more open and connected." This inspiring vision helps employees see how their work contributes to others. Google's mission, "to organize the world's information and make it universally accessible and useful," does the same. While IKEA's vision, "to create a better everyday life for many people," may help an employee feel like their work matters.

Once you have created an inspiring, purpose-filled vision, it is important to then connect the employees' work to that vision. In the IKEA example above, for instance, a leader needs to help employees understand how their home products could "create a better everyday life" for customers. Perhaps the customers' new comforter, pictures, and plants bring warmth and comfort to a lonely college student, making her life better. Or maybe the employee cashier is selling a first sofa to a new homeowner, representing a new beginning. This employee is assisting the customer "create a better everyday life," and a transformative leader will help the employee recognize that. The employee will, in turn, be motivated to work harder, sometimes thinking of creative new ways to help customers.

It is therefore important to share your organization's vision regularly and consistently. The vision should be visually displayed and discussed constantly. You should share the vision in meetings, through email correspondence, and in performance reviews. Employees should be able to recite the vision immediately, and each and every person in the organization should know why they do what they do every day. The work is tied to a larger purpose, and everybody plays a role. Once employees are connected to their role, they should have enhanced engagement and be more likely to create useful and original ideas that propel the organization's vision further.

When we are transformative, creativity will flourish. Employees will work from their strengths and feel understood and supported. They will know your organization's vision and be given opportunities to be challenged. And finally, they will see you as a role model—someone who is creative not just in your organization, but also in your life. With you now at the helm, creativity can flourish.

Reflection Questions

1. Are you modeling creativity in your work? Do you engage in creative problem solving? Do you risk making mistakes by offering out-of-the-box ideas in meetings? Do you still pursue creative interests as an individual? Do you discuss these interests with your staff?

2. Do you individually consider the needs and motivations of each of your staff members, or do you randomly assign them tasks? Can you assign projects more thoughtfully in order to ensure there is a better "fit" in terms of strengths and interests for your followers?

3. Are you challenging your followers to work outside their comfort zones and stretch themselves?

4. Do you offer feedback to your followers on a regular basis and discuss small wins and progress?

5. Is your vision for the organization compelling and communicated on a regular basis? How can you make the vision more alive for your followers?

Notes

1. Grudin, Robert. *The Grace of Great Things: Creativity and Innovation*. New York, NY: Ticknor & Fields, 1990.

2. Ibid.

3. Ibid.

4. Ibid.

5. Ibid.

6. Ibid.

7. Ibid.

8. Johnson, Russ. *Play: The New Leadership Secret that Changes Everything,* 2014.

9. *SHRM® Fun Work Environment Survey.* Society for Human Resource Management. November 2002. www.shrm.org/research/surveyfindings/documents/shrm%20fun%20work%20environment%20survey.pdf

10. Berg, Justin M., Jane E. Dutton, and Amy Wrzesniewski. What is job crafting and why does it matter? 2008. www.bus.umich.edu/Positive/POS-Teaching-and-Learning/ListPOS-Cases.htm

11. Berg, J., Dutton, J. Wrzesniewski, A. (2010). Managing yourself; Turn the Job you have into the job you want. Harvard Business Review; Berg, J., Dutton, J., LoBuglio, N., Wrzesniewski, A. (2013). Job crafting and cultivating positive meaning and identity in work. Advances in Positive Organizational Psychology, Volume 1, 281–302.

12. Impact Creativity. "Theatrics in the Sky: Creativity is Core to Southwest Airlines Success." 2013.

13. Feintzeig, Rachel. "I Don't Have a Job. I Have a Higher Calling." WSJ. February 24, 2015.

14. Semler, Ricardo. "How to Run a Company with (almost) No Rules." Ted.Com. www.ted.com/talks/ricardo_semler_radical_wisdom_for_a_company_a_school_a_life?language=en

15. Amabile, Theresa. "The Power of Small Wins." *Harvard Business Review.* May 1, 2011.

16. Ibid.

CHAPTER 5

Cultures that Enhance Creativity and Change

Most people have fears and inhibitions that prevent us from excelling and being creative. These fears include fear of failure, fear of others' envy, and fear of disappointing others.[1] These sorts of feelings can be crippling and stifle creativity.

As leaders, we must help our employees grapple with fear and create a culture that brings out the best in our workers. Unfortunately, many leaders do the opposite, creating cultures where risk-taking is discouraged and failure is not acceptable. This is a crucial mistake that will minimize growth and creativity in an organization. Creativity cannot thrive if

- **Employees do not have access to the latest tools, trainings, and information**. After all, how can we expect them to create new ideas if they don't even have an opportunity to learn about the latest ideas?
- **Employees do not have access to diverse perspectives**. We cannot expect employees to awaken to fresh ideas if they work in a closed, sheltered culture with individuals who all think alike.
- **Employees do not have some surplus energy to develop new ideas**. We cannot expect them to thrive if they are overworked and in "drained survival mode." Think about it: while cramming for important finals in college, would you have been able to come up with new and novel ideas to transform an organization?
- **Employees are not allowed to fail**. Would you try something new if failure led to severe punishment or even loss of your job?
- **Employees have no flexibility and freedom**. We cannot expect employees to develop something new if they do not have time and space to work on new tasks.

Ken Robinson, a noted speaker on creativity, has said, "You can't just give someone a creativity injection. You have to create an environment for curiosity and a way to encourage people and get the best out of them."[2]

In order to create this environment, we must pay attention to the physical environment where the employees work (see Chapter 7), as well as the values and assumptions that employees hold in an organization. Edgar Schein, a leading scholar on leadership and culture, classifies an organization's culture into three distinct levels: artifacts, values, and assumptions.[3]

Artifacts are obvious elements of an organization that typically can be seen even to an outsider. The office layout, dress code, posted visions, and free food in the cafeteria are all artifacts that send a message about the overall culture of an organization. Artifacts and space are crucial components of creativity and addressed in Chapter 7.

The espoused values, or declared set of **values** and norms of an organization, directly influence culture and affect how members interact and work in the organization. Values are standards and principles that guide an organization's behaviors and beliefs. Most companies have a list of core values. Some even reinforce these values publicly on office walls or through regular communications within the organization.

An organization's declared values influence creativity. If the organization lists risk-taking and collaboration as a key value, employees may feel motivated to develop creative ideas or work with new teams. On the other hand, if profit, success, and customer service are the **only** listed values of an organization, then employees may believe they should not spend their time developing new ideas: doing so could take "time away" from short-term profit and customer satisfaction.

Zappos is an online retailer that prides itself on living its core values. Zappos believes these values are fundamental to its success and mandates memorization of the values by employees. The ten core values of Zappos are:

1. Deliver WOW through service
2. Embrace and drive change
3. Create fun and a little weirdness
4. Be adventurous, creative, and open-minded
5. Pursue growth and learning
6. Build open and honest relationships with communication

7. Build a positive team and family spirit
8. Do more with less
9. Be passionate and determined
10. Be humble

This list tells employees and customers something about the organization: we know employees can take risks, drive change, and be creative. We also know that employees should seek continuous improvement and build strong relationships at work. They should be passionate and determined but also humble—all key characterizes of strong creative types.

Zappos stated values work, in part because they are written, stated, and shared. However, the values would mean nothing if they were not honored as part of Zappos' overall culture. In fact, "stated" values are useless when they do not clearly align with acceptable behaviors in an organization. For instance, an organization that condemns different ideas will not be seen as one that values creativity and open-mindedness, even **if** those values are written on the walls. Actions speak louder than words, and create shared assumptions about the true values of an organization.

Shared basic **assumptions** form the bedrock of culture in an organization. They are the deeply embedded beliefs of an organization: they represent what employees really believe about the organization's values and priorities. Sometimes, basic assumptions are reflected in the stated values. For instance, employees may truly believe the leaders want them to collaborate if the organization discusses the need to collaborate regularly, rewards teams rather than individuals, and has open spaces for collaboration. On the other hand, employees may assume that risk-taking is discouraged when they are punished for failure, even if risk-taking is "discussed" as a value of the company.

Zappos not only shares core values, they live their core values. Every employee memorizes the values and talks about them. They want employees committed to the values of the organization and will pay to ensure engaged commitment. For instance, if a new employee does not believe in the core values, Zappos will pay that person over $1,000 to quit. Since they believe in creating fun and weirdness, employees regularly have parties and share pictures of the latest company celebration on their blog. The organization promotes life-long learning by giving employees a dedicated library to check out preferred books and lives its core value of team spirit through the Holacracy system. This system of teamwork removes traditional hierarchies and allows employees to self-organize to complete their work.

By creating these stated values and living them, Zappos succeeds in engaging employees and bringing creativity to the workplace. Leaders work to create a culture where the values are not just stated, but alive. This culture takes time, energy, and commitment. But is brings results, engagement, and creativity.

Try It Yourself

In this try-it-yourself exercise, we will be reflecting on your organization's core values. It is important to be honest and thoughtful when answering the questions below. Take out a pen and paper and begin writing the following:

- What are your organization's core values?
  - If you do not have a set of 5 to 10 core statements that declare your organization's values, it is time to begin drafting them. Make a list of 5 to 10 of the values you believe your organization should hold dear. Share and discuss this list with trusted colleagues, and refine your draft until you have a list that speaks to you and your organization.
  - If you do have a set of core values, do they resonate with the organization and its employees? Does the list make sense? Does it promote a culture that will enhance creativity or diminish it? Does it encourage risk-taking, bold thinking, and excellence?
- Once you have a strong set of core values, consider posting them publicly and speak about them often.
- As the leader, ask everyone in the company to memorize the values and reward those who speak about the values often.
- Think about whether your employees truly believe your organization lives by its core values. How can you make your core values more pronounced in your organization?

As seen by Zappos' example, it is crucial to not only state core values, but also live them. After all, if our culture does not send the right message, we could be paralyzed by fear and unable to develop new and useful ideas and tools. Leaders need to help remove our personal inhibitions in order to enhance creativity within organizations. To do so, they must instill key assumptions into the culture of our organizations.

For many years, researchers have been exploring ways to enhance creativity and effectiveness in organizations. Several key assumptions have stood out as ones that help organizations grow in productivity and creativity. Some of these key assumptions are as follows:

- We believe that risk and mistakes are okay and even encouraged.
- We value playfulness and celebrate success.
- We value flexibility and time off.
- We have a thoughtful, fair reward system based on a number of factors that extend beyond just success and profit.
- We respect our employees and give them autonomy.
- We challenge ourselves and others in the organization.
- We support each other, collaborate, and ensure that everyone has needed resources for priority projects.
- We do not promote overwhelm or burnout.
- We hire diverse people who all share a common spirit: They want to excel and be challenged and creative in some way.
- We encourage thoughtful feedback and take well-timed criticism as an opportunity to grow and improve our work.
- We value each member of our team and celebrate their victories: Ego is not welcome in our organization.

Failure Is Accepted in Our Organization

Few people will try new ideas if they are punished for failure. Yet every creative idea has the potential for failure or success. So, if you want to enhance creativity, you must send a message that risk-taking and smart failure is acceptable.

Writing for *Harvard Business Review*, Peter Sims says the number one enemy of creativity is fear of failure. In the article, Sims says,

> If you're an MBA-trained manager or executive, the odds are you were never, at any point in your educational or professional career, given permission to fail, even on a "little bet." Your parents wanted you to achieve, achieve, achieve—in sports, the classroom, and scouting or work. Your teachers penalized you for having the "wrong" answers, or knocked your grades down if you were imperfect, according to however your adult figures defined perfection. Similarly, modern industrial management is still predicated largely on mitigating risks and preventing errors, not innovating or inventing.
>
> But entrepreneurs and designers think of failure the way most people think of learning. As Darden Professor Sara Sarasvathy has shown through her research about how expert entrepreneurs make decisions, they must make lots of mistakes to discover new approaches, opportunities, or business models. She frequently references Howard Schultz who, when he started Il Giornale in Seattle, the company that Schultz used to later buy the original Starbucks brand and assets, the store had nonstop opera music playing, menus written in Italian, and no chairs. As Schultz has often said, "We had to make a lot of mistakes" before discovering a model that worked.[4]

Mistakes will happen at the origination of a business, as it did in Howard Schultz's case. Then, fear of failure can be crippling. But fear of failure can also be pronounced as businesses become larger and more successful. After all, there is more to lose if a successful company publically fails.

Fear of failure is to be expected. But creativity cannot thrive if employees are paralyzed by fear. Thus, leaders must create an environment of safety, convincing people that they will not be punished or humiliated if they speak up with ideas or make mistakes. Unsuccessful trials offer a rich potential for creative learning and can lead to success in time.

History has shown that mistakes can bring great success. Thomas Edison conducted thousands of experiments before he successfully invented the incandescent bulb. He did not view these "experiments" as failure. He said, "I have not failed. I've just found 10,000 ways that won't work." Edison also said, "Many of life's failures are people who did not realize how close they were to success when they gave up."

This is often the case in our organizations. Leaders penalize and shame those who fail, and employees stop taking risks and sharing new ideas. As leaders, we must turn this around and create a culture where failure is acceptable. To do so, you should consider the following actions:

- Talk about personal failures and how those failures enhanced you as an individual
- Talk about organizational failures and discuss how those failures led to new learnings and knowledge
- Consider adopting "bravery," "experimentation," and/ or "playfulness" as a core value and include a phrase about mistakes in this value. For instance, "We value employees who bravely share and create new concepts and ideas. We reward success and failure, and believe both are keys to effective growth"
- Use rewards appropriately (see below).
- Use feedback appropriately (see below).

We Reward Effort, Success, and Failure

Time and again, research has shown that monetary bonuses do not enhance motivation or even success if the individual is able to live comfortably and makes a fair salary.[5] In fact, money can sometimes diminish motivation. In a recent study, researchers offered participants a lottery ticket that gave them a chance to win an $80 gym membership for every second that they held a plank. "Subjects who exercised with a partner and had this extrinsic incentive held planks half as long as those with no opportunity for lottery tickets. The incentive seemed to fight with their intrinsic motivation. It created competing goals—help the team or get a gym membership—and distracted them from the more powerful motivation."[6]

Surely, rewards for creativity *can* enhance drive and motivation. But giving an employee extra money to complete "good work" typically does not lead to innovative or creative work. "When people are told that rewards are for merely completing or participating in a task or when people receive prior rewards for output irrespective of its creativity, creativity tends to decrease or, at the least, not increase."[7]

As a leader then, it is important to carefully consider offering rewards for execution and completion of ideas. We want employees to feel internally motivated to perform. If the employee begins to perform solely for rewards, then the outcome may suffer. Thus, a leader should work to develop other ways to motivate followers intrinsically (see Chapter 4) and carefully scrutinize when it is appropriate to give rewards based on **execution**.

However, rewards for the **generation** of creative ideas can, at times, be motivating. Video game developer Frima Studio believes in rewarding employees in this way and created Frima Points to do just that. With Frima Points, employees are given points when they share a small new idea. These points can later be traded for tangible gifts like payment for babysitters or home repair services. Great ideas are also recognized monthly at RockYou, a social game developing and advertising company. Driven by peer nominations, RockYou awards are given to employees for solving a problem, designing a game, or otherwise showing innovation.

This enhanced reward system is typically not practiced at most organizations. Generally speaking, employees are given a reward or bonus for bringing in new business or profit. And while rewards make sense in those cases, it is also important to grow your employees' intrinsic motivation. You should carefully consider how your current reward system enhances and impedes creativity, and work to:

- Reward ideas, not just action
- Offer a variety of different rewards, including days off, flexible time, tickets to shows, and trinket trophies that could be a symbol of pride in the organization
- Reward "hard work" for complex projects when morale and motivation is low

- Use public recognition as a form of reward: acknowledge great ideas and creative thinkers in meetings and newsletters
- Be like Zappos and consider peer-to-peer rewards. Here, employees award bonuses to their colleagues for excellent work or creativity
- Think about VIP rewards for excellent innovators and creators. Perhaps give them a VIP parking space or feature them on your company website

We Value and Encourage Play in Our Organization

We have already seen that playfulness is a common characteristic of creative individuals, and we've recognized that transformational leaders should cultivate playfulness as a habit. In Chapter 7, we will discuss the value of creating playful, collaborative spaces. However, none of that will matter if the organizational culture discourages playfulness.

A person who is naturally playful at home will temper that characteristic if such behavior is frowned upon at work. And a newbie will not be vulnerable enough to express playfulness if that behavior is not expressly valued and practiced in the organization. Organizations must, therefore, value, express, and encourage playfulness in every aspect of the culture.

As an organizational leader, you can formally express this value and instill it in your employees. You can share jokes in office meetings and go out with the team purely for fun in the middle of the day on occasion. As well, you could consider running brainstorming sessions or contests that let people play and think outside the box. Basketball hoops over doors, games in conference rooms, and quotes on the walls can show employees that "this firm is playful" and it is "okay" to have fun at work. Trainings can include Legos or improv (see Chapter 8) that again solidify this playful value. Perhaps you even do something quite different to be playful. You could

- Host a 10 minute "out-of-this-world" idea session where employees dream up the worst possible solution to a current client issue
- Hold a "Top Chef" like contest for the best baker in the office over lunch

- Host an activity like indoor skydiving or paintball instead of your typical holiday party

Playfulness is often a prerequisite to creative, new solutions and ideas. Therefore, it should be valued and practiced regularly in a creative, strong organization.

We Give Our Employees Flexibility and Autonomy

Many leaders direct their followers on a daily basis. The employees report to work by 8 a.m., leave at 5 p.m. or later, and are given two to three weeks of vacation and sick time a year. They are paid for their work, but given little autonomy, flexibility, and freedom. This results in overworked, spent employees who eventually disengage, lose motivation, and fail to develop new creative ideas.

The research is rather clear: An employee who is micromanaged and given little autonomy and flexibility will not be as creative or motivated as one who is given time and space to complete work.[8] So, if you want a creative, energized office, you must give employees flexibility and autonomy. The employees need time and space to play, prepare, learn, and develop new ideas. As a leader, it is important to give employees time to incubate and let the creative process unfold. As well, giving employees freedom over their schedules can bring newfound energy, motivation and creativity.

Unfortunately, leaders often feel hesitant to give employees independence and flexibility because they fear that it will lead to ineffectiveness and detachment. Theresa Amabile has done a great deal of research on autonomy and says:

> When people are well matched to a project, granting them independence holds less risk. Ideally, creative workers would be able to set their own agendas, at least in part. The practice of letting researchers spend a significant percentage of their time on projects of their own choosing was famously employed by 3M in its high-growth era. Google's decision to do the same has yielded new offerings like Google Scholar.[9]

Try It Yourself

It is bold and scary to give your employees flexibility, autonomy, and time off. However, most people sense that time away from the office, email, and computer can be energizing, and that flexibility and autonomy can be powerful motivators. So, give your employees flexibility. Let them create their own schedule, at least in part, and watch their motivation and gratitude increase. Here are a few ideas to get you started:

- Consider setting aside a "disconnect" time, where employees are not able to work or check email. Build in anautoresponder message for emails during this time and watch engagement and your overall culture improve.
- Consider letting employees set their own schedule for "office time." Some organizations find that required office hours between 10 a.m. and 2 p.m. allow time for collaboration and meetings but also empower employees to set their own schedule. This autonomy lets people work longer hours when motivated and engaged while truly giving them a chance to recharge when feeling uninspired.

Autonomy and flexibility give employees time to problem solve and develop new and useful ideas. Steve Jobs recognized that time was needed to solve complex problems, stating "When you first start off trying to solve a problem, the first solutions you come up with are very complex, and most people stop there. But if you keep going, and live with the problem and peel more layers of the onion off, you can often times arrive at some very elegant and simple solutions."[10]

Zahra Ebrahim, professor and founder and principal of archiTEXT, believes in the power of flexibility and time off. She writes, "The negotiation between 'having to do' and 'loving to do' is something that I have struggled with." Ebrahim encourages students to unplug, take sabbaticals, and work to connect with what they really love. She implemented a summer sabbatical at her firm, saying, "I knew that if we continued to work at a 12-hour-a-day pace, both the quality of our work, and our love for its practice, diminish. If an email is sent during this sabbatical, an automatic response is generated saying, 'We give your entire team the summer off to go on a creative journey, to rejuvenate, to reconnect to ideas that make them tick.' It makes our work better, it makes our ideas richer, and makes our jobs feel more like dream jobs." During her summer sabbatical, Ebrahim studied improvisation at 2nd City and found the experience rewarding and rejuvenating. It also recharged her, improving her work and engagement in the fall.[11]

We Encourage Thoughtful Feedback and Take Well-Timed Criticism as an Opportunity to Grow and Improve Our Work

Feedback can make or break creativity and engagement. Given too soon, it can halt new ideas. But if one waits too long, then lack of feedback can diminish motivation and engagement.

Our employees want feedback. In fact, 50 percent of high performers say they expect at least a monthly sit down with their managers. Unfortunately, less than 50 percent of these high performers say their manager delivers on feedback expectations.[12] Thus, it is important to deliver feedback rather regularly.

However, we should let ideas flow before giving too much criticism. That way, people will feel free to share ideas. Once ideas have been shared and initially developed, then feedback can be crucial to not only increase motivation, but also enhance the result.

Timing is one important key to effective feedback, but tone is another. Most people have been the recipient of terrible feedback that halted all engagement: The feedback was targeted and mean-spirited. As a strong leader, you should deliver thoughtful feedback that is aimed at improving the work. Brene Brown, a leading scholar and best-selling author, has worked with leaders all around the world. She has created a feedback manifesto on this topic. This feedback manifesto says,

I know I am ready to give feedback when:

- *I'm ready to sit next to you rather than across from you.*
- *I'm willing to put the problem in front of us rather than between us (or sliding it toward you).*

- *I'm ready to listen and ask questions, and accept that I may not fully understand the issue.*
- *I want to acknowledge what you do well instead of picking apart your mistakes.*
- *I recognize your strengths and how you can use them to address your challenges.*
- *I can hold you accountable without shaming or blaming you.*
- *I'm willing to own my part.*
- *I can genuinely thank you for your efforts rather than criticize you for your failings.*
- *I can talk about how resolving these challenges will lead to your growth and opportunity.*
- *I can model the vulnerability and openness that I expect to see from you.*[13]

If you deliver feedback using those concepts, you will not only show respect for the recipient, but also portray fairness and compassion. The recipient of your thoughtful feedback will know that it was given out of care and concern, not blame. Surely, feedback given in that manner will be more effective overall.

It is important to give feedback in a compassionate way. Equally important, though, is accepting feedback. If you take feedback personally, your followers will as well. Thus, it is important to:

- Listen thoughtfully to feedback and look at it as an opportunity to grow.
- Thank the other person for giving you feedback.
- Remember the benefits of feedback: It is meant to help you and the organization grow.
- Ask clarifying questions like "How would you have done it differently?" or "What would success look like in this situation?"
- Take time to think over the feedback. It is perfectly acceptable to say, "Thank you very much for the feedback. I'd like to think about it."

We Work to Ensure Employees Have Support and Resources to Succeed

Employees who are underresourced will not succeed. They will be overworked and lack energy to excel and thrive. If you want successful creative outcomes, you must ensure that employees have resources and tools to achieve those outcomes and work productively. Sometimes, this means organizations need to cut projects and/or reallocate resources. And while this can be risky, it is also risky to continue to burn out employees and not give them resources they need to deliver outstanding results.

Try It Yourself

A leading scholar on authentic leadership, Robert Terry, says that leaders must explore "what is really, really going on in an organization."[14] Sometimes, merely asking that question leads to astonishing revelations that can transform effectiveness and creativity.

Let's explore the question in relationship to workload and resources. To do so, talk to a few employees and ask them about their workload and top two to three projects. Then ask the following:

- Are these two to three projects a true priority for the organization? Why?
- Are you given enough assistance, training, funding, and time to complete these top projects?
- What other projects are on your plates, and how do these projects enhance the organization?

Then, ask yourself the following:

- Should you remove projects and tasks from this employee's list?
- Do you need to reallocate resources or projects to help this employee succeed?
- How might lack of resources be contributing to this employee's work product and overall engagement?

A strong creative organization will give employees resources to succeed and make reallocations and cuts in order to ensure their success.

We Value Each Member of Our Team and Celebrate Personal and Group Victories

Creative individuals are collaborators. They recognize their key strengths and know they are imperfect. Their creative results are made possible because of collaboration, teamwork, and feedback, together with passion for the work.

Successful creative organizations know that ego and pride do not mix with successful creative outcomes. Every individual has valid, useful ideas and potential. Each individual should have a chance to be heard, and every project should be about the project, not the person whose name is attached to the project.

At Foursquare, the company behind the location-aware app of the same name, employees in its New York City office showcase ideas equally on demo days. On these demo days, held every couple of weeks, people at the company of all levels and titles demonstrate concepts they've been working on to the rest of the company. This equal sharing enables all members of the organization to participate in its success, not just a few.

When we only celebrate a few employees, others lose motivation and fail to contribute. Thus, it is vital to create mechanisms whereby every employee has a voice and is valued. There is not one superstar in a highly creative organization: rather, each employee is a star in your shared galaxy (your organization).

In the end, a strong creative leader will consciously create a culture that promotes creativity and risk-taking. In the right culture, people will be more engaged and creative, leading to better outcomes. And when they are more engaged, they will collaborate more often, leading to even better creative results.

Reflection Questions

To determine whether you are creating a strong culture to enhance creativity, ask yourself the following questions:

1. How would you describe your current culture?
    a. Does your organization promote risk-taking?
    b. How do you reward success and failure?
    c. What kind of flexibility do employees have?
    d. How is feedback delivered?

2. What are your personal values? Do you live those values?

3. What are your organization's values? Can you recite them by heart? Does your organization live those values?

4. What, do you believe, your followers would say you value? Would your followers say that your actions align with your values? Would they say your actions align with your organization's values?

5. What can you do this week to create a culture where people feel free to develop and share creative ideas?

6. What can you do this month to create a culture where people feel free to develop and share creative ideas?

Notes

1. Barron, Carrie, and Alton Barron. *The Creativity Cure: A Do-it-yourself Prescription for Happiness*. New York, NY: Scribner, 2012.

2. Scanlon, Jessica. "Reading, Writing, and Creativity." Bloomberg. com. February 22, 2006.

3. Schein, E. (2010). Organizational Culture and Leadership.

4. Sims, Peter. "The No. 1 Enemy of Creativity: Fear of Failure." *Harvard Business Review.* October 5, 2012. https://hbr.org/2012/10/the-no-1-enemy-of-creativity-f

5. Amabile, "The Power of Small Wins."; Gladwell, Malcolm. *Outliers: The Story of Success*. Boston: Little, Brown and Company, 2008.

6. Irwin, Brandon. "If You Want to Motivate Someone, Shut Up Already." *Harvard Business Review.* July 1, 2013. https://hbr.org/2013/07/if-you-want-to-motivate-someone-shut-up-already

7. Rewards and Creativity. R Eisenberger, University of Houston, Houston, TX, USA; K Byron, Syracuse University, Syracuse, NY, USA © 2011 Elsevier Inc. All rights reserved. (Encyclopedia of Creativity). www.psychology.uh.edu/faculty/Eisenberger/files/rewards-and-creat.pdf

8. Amabile, "The Power of Small Wins."; Pink, *A Whole New Mind: Why Right-brainers Will Rule the Future.*

9. Amabile, Theresa. "Creativity and the Role of the Leader." *Harvard Business Review.* October 1, 2008.

10. Jobs, Steve, and George W. Beahm. *I, Steve Steve Jobs, in His Own Words*. Chicago: B2 Books, 2011.

11. Ebrahim, Zahra. "Sagmeister Was Right: We Need Time Off." The Huffington Post. August 26, 2013.

12. Willyerd, Karie. "What High Performers Want at Work." *Harvard Business Review.* November 18, 2014.

13. Brown, Brene. *Daring Greatly: How the Courage to Be Vulnerable Transforms the Way We Live, Love, Parent, and Lead*. New York, NY: Gotham Books, 2012.

14. Quinn, Robert E. *Deep Change: Discovering the Leader within*. San Francisco, CA: Jossey-Bass Publishers, 1996.

CHAPTER 6

Collaboration

The Key to Enhanced Creativity

We often think that creative people work in isolation. We hear stories about lonely artists, writers, and inventors and suspect that they are geniuses working alone. Yet research shows that collaboration enhances creativity.

Why Collaborate?

More and more, businesses are forced to collaborate in today's economy. We are interconnected globally, and our workforce is composed of multiple generations. We are called to work together with others, and collaboration is a requirement of many jobs in the 21st-century. Thus, it is important to learn to collaborate effectively, and embrace the idea of collaboration.

Research shows that it is smart to collaborate.[1] Collaboration may lead to:

- **A greater number of ideas, since more people are offering input.**
- **A more successful, useful product or idea.** Input from others helps us see the flaws of our ideas. We can use collaboration as a tool to refine our ideas and make them more realistic and useful.
- **A reframed problem or refocused lens on the issue.** Sometimes, we work on a problem for endless hours only to find that we were working on the wrong problem in the first place. We may have developed a brilliant marketing campaign, but lack the motivation in our employees to make our campaign a reality. When we

collaborate, others may help us reprioritize, and show us that our top priority should be people management, not marketing.

For Writers

Editors work to modify, tweak, and improve writers' words. Books, articles, and even poems are completed through collaboration between the writer, editor, and others. This collaboration brings new insight, feedback, and ideas, and ultimately enhances the final product.

But writers often work on their first draft in collaboration with others as well. Writers groups, conferences, and associations are growing in popularity. In these settings, writers can get a better feel of their audience, get feedback on their work, and have others hold them accountable.

"The Inklings" is one such example. This group of British writers included J. R. R. Tolkien, C. S. Lewis, Charles Williams, and many other prominent authors and poets of the time. They held regular meetings to connect with and support each other. In the meetings, they often shared their latest drafts of novels or poems. Most of the shared content was a work in progress that the group helped move forward. For instance, legend has it that Tolkien did not believe the manuscript he'd been reading at meetings (*The Lord of the Rings*) was strong enough for publication, but C. S. Lewis convinced him to submit it.

For Business Creatives

Sometimes, joining forces with other organizations and diverse individuals in business can yield greater success and creativity. When you collaborate with other marketing experts, you may learn new methods and models to enhance your approaches. Collaborating with other businesses could result in a new service offering. And employee development plans can be improved when those in your human resources group work with other organizations to learn best practices in leadership and creativity.

Michael Engelman is constantly seeking new and useful ways to market media as executive vice-president of marketing, digital, and global brand strategy at Syfy Channel, which aired *Sharknado* as well as *Battlestar*

Galatica. Engelman says that "great ideas come from collaboration." When he is in a creative rut, he says it is "helpful to work with different people or change around the team. There's a great generational convergence happening where the tried and true vets are working side-by-side with these whiz kids. You need that experience in convert with wide-eyed eagerness of just starting out."[2]

For Artists

Artists regularly collaborate with others. Through art schools, they are able to learn and get feedback from experts. These relationships often persist past school and provide a forum to continue to learn, grow, and improve.

Andy Warhol and Jean-Michel Basquiat partnered together for a couple of years in the 1980s and demonstrated the value of collaboration. Warhol's biographer said the relationship was "like some crazy art-world marriage. The relationship was symbiotic. Jean-Michel (the more novice artist) thought he needed Andy's fame and Andy thought he needed Jean-Michel's new blood."[3] Jean-Michel convinced Warhol to paint on canvas again, while Warhol helped Jean-Michel experiment with new art mediums like silkscreen printing. In the end, the collaboration inspired each artist to stretch in new ways and enhanced their overall creations.[4]

Collaboration is crucial to success in the performing arts as well. Without lights and sound, even an Oscar-winning actor will fail. As well, it is the director's job to work collaboratively with a wide range of personalities in order to stage a winning play.

For Researchers

More and more academics are collaborating on their research projects. They work on small teams, often within a university or through collaborative intercollegiate meetings. This collaboration proves quite successful. As the number of authors on a paper increases, the number of citations also increases, and more citations equate with a more influential and higher quality research paper. In the end, team-authored research papers are cited 2.1 times as often as solo projects.[5]

Collaboration works. It enhances our engagement, our services and our products. Interestingly, the mere presence of people can enhance performance and creativity. In 1920, social psychologist Flloyd Allport showed that a group of people working individually at the same table performed better than those working alone in a room. The energy of those at the table seemed to enhance creativity, even when they did not officially work together. Thus, it is not surprising that many creatives find their best work happens in buzzing cafes and shared office spaces. For them, the energy and noise level in social settings enhances creativity.[6]

What Is Collaboration?

Working near others is not the same as collaborating **with** others. Collaboration involves working with someone to produce or create something. It may involve teamwork throughout the entirety of a project. Or, it may involve a smaller commitment such as collaborating with others for feedback on a portion of a project.

There are several different types of collaboration. Gary Pisano, professor of business at Harvard Business School, and Robert Vergante, professor of management of innovation at Politecnico di Milano, assert that there are four different types of collaboration.[7]

- **Innovation Mall:** This is a hierarchical mode of collaboration when a company or individual posts a problem, allowing anyone to suggest a solution. With Innovation Mall collaboration, the company decides which ideas to ultimately develop.

  Innovation mall can help creatives find new and useful methods, ideas, and solutions to problems. For example, imagine a creative entrepreneur who wants to develop a new marketing campaign for her values-based coaching business. She creates a call for help on social media and asks others to give her ideas. People from all over share the call for help, and anyone or everyone can offer input. In the end, some of the ideas are good, but some were unrealistic and misguided. The entrepreneur can use as

many or as few of the ideas presented and retains full
control over implementation.

- **Innovation Community:** This is an open mode of
collaboration within a network where anyone can propose
problems, offer solutions, and decide which solutions
are developed. Linux open-source software employs this
type of collaboration. At Linux, a community of people
discusses problems and solutions, and develops software to
fix the problems.

  In this type of collaboration, the values-based coach
would again ask others for help to create a marketing
campaign. This time, the collaborators would be within a
network and perhaps have more experience and/or insight
than with innovation mall. The collaborators may create some
brilliant work. But again, because it is an "open mode" of
collaboration, some may be truly off the mark. In the end, the
originator of the project retains control over execution.

- **Elite Circle:** This is a closed and hierarchical mode of
collaboration. Here, a company or individual posits a problem,
and a select group of participants will work to develop
solutions. The solution is chosen by the company or individual.

  In this type of collaboration, the values-based coach may,
for instance, ask 10 other coaches and 10 marketing experts for
assistance on her campaign. She would then review the input
from this closed field of collaborators while retaining authority
to decide on the result. The input will be targeted and relevant
since it comes from a group of collaborators with some expertise.

- **Closed, Flat Collaboration or "Consortium":** This occurs
when a private group of participants select problems together,
decide how to work, and choose solutions.

  In closed collaboration, the values-based coach would
share her business model with a select group of individuals.
Together, they may decide that marketing is her greatest
need and create a strong campaign. However, they may also
reframe and reprioritize, deciding that she needs to focus on
her vision and values first, before developing a marketing

campaign. This sort of collaboration helps expand the coach's frame of reference and allows her to refocus on the most important issues.

Each type of collaboration can be useful to enhance creativity.

Try It Yourself

Think about each of the four types of collaboration. What sort of collaboration do you think would work best for you, and why? What would work worst? Then, try collaborating with your preferred and least-preferred form of collaboration.

First, develop a one-paragraph summary of your nonconfidential problem. End your paragraph telling participants that you are looking for new ideas to help solve your problem.

Then, directly ask participants for input and assure them that some of the "worst" ideas initially turn into the best solutions over time.

- For Innovation Mall: Go on Facebook or ask a friend to send an email request to his/her friends posting your paragraph. See what sort of responses you get and try to find a golden nugget in some of the ideas.
- For Innovation Community: Share your paragraph through a professional association or an online, targeted group (LinkedIn has some targeted groups for a variety of industries and interests).
- For Elite Circle: Share your paragraph with a small group of experts in your field. Be sure to look outside of your organization.
- For Closed Collaboration: Share your paragraph with a closed group of experts, but also tell them you are open to reframing the entire issue and/or exploring other issues to enhance success. Encourage participants to look at your entire business with fresh eyes, and see if they can develop a list of problems that they believe you face, as well as some solutions.

Some pros and cons for each type are listed in Chart 5.1.

Chart 5.1 Types of Collaboration

	Innovation mall	Innovation community	Elite circle	Closed collaboration (consortium)
Strengths	• A broad range of ideas are offered, leading to new ideas never previously considered • Diverse concepts are suggested, enhancing the chance that some "nugget" of wisdom is offered that can move the creation or change forward	• The network provides some consistency, but is also balanced by a broad range of thinkers • Outside perspectives bring additional ideas to the table • Outside perspectives add to the number of ideas and can enhance "out of the box" thinking	• Targeted, expert advice can lead to solid workable solutions • Knowledge of the consortium enhances the ideas • Input from others brings new ideas and helps refine existing ideas	• Targeted, expert advice can lead to novel, relevant, and workable solutions in a timely fashion • The consortium is willing to reframe the entire issue at hand and may develop relevant creative solutions never before considered
Weaknesses	• Too much time is spent parring out irrelevant ideas • In some cases, few, if any, good ideas are presented at all • Time, focus, and money are wasted that move the person or business away from change and/or creation	• Too much time is spent parring out irrelevant ideas • Too many ideas are presented, making it difficult to find any useful options at all	• An elite group may fail to produce true "out of the box" ideas • Because they work so close to the issue at hand on a daily basis, the elite group may fail to see that the entire problem needs to be reframed	• A closed consortium may fail to produce true "out of the box" ideas because they already have expertise and knowledge. Sometimes, an outsider is needed to bring true novelty • Without an outsider, they may fail to see the real issue at hand

What Not to Do

Group work can be highly successful. However, key mistakes are regularly made with teamwork and collaboration, creating complications and sometimes resulting in less effective products and services. These mistakes can include:

- **Randomly assigning people to a team** and hoping the collaboration will be magical. At a minimum, participants must be motivated and engaged, and random assignments usually result in placement of some who do not want to be part of the team.
- **Numerous "meetings"** that often reduce motivation and limit the team's ability to share information in an engaging, passionate way. When overdone, meetings become additional chores and collaboration is less successful.
- **Allowing one superstar to do the vast majority of the work.**
- **Encouraging one superstar to overshare**, thereby limiting the amount of time others may feel comfortable sharing.
- **Regularly evaluating individual members of the team** for their contributions or lack thereof, making them hesitant to offer ideas for fear they may be "wrong."
- **Exclusive focus on commonalities**, rather than unique differences and expertise.
- **Jumping on the first idea in a collaborative meeting**, rather than working to develop subsequent ideas.
- **Not giving the team autonomy and freedom** to explore novel ideas.
- **Failing to create an environment where participants feel free and safe to share all ideas.**[8]
- **Keeping all meetings in the office conference room, or worse, in one participant's office.**

Leadership that Works: Enhancing Collaboration

As a leader, it is important to create opportunities for collaboration in your organization. In order to enhance creativity and collaboration, you should do the following:

- **Model collaboration by being an active member of associations, groups, and networks outside of your organization**

   A wide circle of colleagues can provide referrals, information, and developmental support. Members of associations may inform you about recent trends, keep you up-to-date on advancements in the industry, or guide you toward a new future. If you remain insular and do not collaborate outside of your organization, you will probably miss key trends and advancements, creating stagnation and stalling creativity.[9]

- **Share ideas with a broad range of individuals within your organization**

   As a creator and leader, you should seek input and advice from a broad and diverse range of people. It is important to openly share knowledge and information about your work and projects and solicit feedback from a variety of teams and employees within your organization. Open knowledge sharing in this way brings new perspectives and ideas and ultimately enhances the organization.

   Pixar is known for this type of collaboration when producing films. Pixar's operating principles state the following:

   1. Everyone must have freedom to communicate with anyone.
   2. It must be safe for everyone to offer ideas.

   Pixar's success is based, in part, on these principles. Employees are able to approach anyone, at any level, in another department to solve problems. Hierarchy is not a barrier, and collaboration across teams is encouraged.[10]

• **Create diverse work teams**
Some creative work can begin independently. But often, teams are needed to develop business, bring in new ideas, and implement projects.

Many leaders create teams randomly. Other teams may be created due to position, rank, or group within an organization. Many of these teams will work together for years on a project. Unfortunately, those methods of creating teams are not best for enhancing creativity and change.

Several of the most creative companies build diverse teams made up of individuals with varying educational backgrounds, expertise, and experiences. Then, they regularly rotate team members to bring even more diverse ideas to the table.

This sort of collaboration is commonplace at Menlo, Inc., a successful software business known for its innovation. At Menlo, employees of varying experiences work in pairs on a shared computer. At the end of the week, they switch partners and possibly projects. The CEO believes that this sort of collaboration enhances problem solving, brings in new perspectives, and creates strong mentoring opportunities within the company. He says, "We borrowed the idea of switching from the airline industry. The National Transportation Safety Bureau realized many years ago that if a pilot and copilot work together a lot it breeds a complacency that produces danger. Their minds no longer inject the questioning, the curiosity, the 'Hey, why are you doing it like this?' Switching gives us that freshness."[11]

Like Menlo, Nissan relies on diverse, cross-functional teams to help promote creative solutions. The organization creates teams using a variety of different professionals from a range of groups and geographical regions. The diverse

teams are brought together to solve problems, create
new ways of thinking, and reconsider current business
processes. The teams provide fresh thinking and vision for
the company on issues of cost, quality, design, profit, and
other goals, like creating a genderless organization. And
the diverse teams have worked to make the company more
successful.

Your organization can work collaboratively as well if
you take the lead to initiate these working relationships.
Sometimes, it may be best to diversify your work teams
by bringing in new, passionate employees from a variety
of sectors. Creating diverse teams in this way may lead to
new perspectives and fresh ideas, sparking creativity and
innovation in your work.

- **Bring in outsiders to share opinions on ideas**
  Outsiders often bring a fresh eye that may not exist within
  your organization. They do not fully comprehend your
  organization's history or obstacles, allowing them to see
  things with a different perspective than "insiders." Because of
  that, outsiders may be able to develop new ideas that spark
  something original and useful for your team.

  Sometimes, these outsiders may be your competition
  or a closely related company or leader. This is the case with
  Nissan, whose success is enhanced because they partner
  with another car manufacturer, Renault, to continue to
  develop fresh, creative solutions to business problems. For
  instance, Renualt and Nissan have worked together to tackle
  the problem of rising raw material prices, since both have a
  common interest in this cause. For three months, the teams
  from Nissan and Renault worked on this issue. In the end,
  they created more than 15 initiatives to reduce raw material
  costs by several hundred million euros, benefiting both
  companies.[12]

  Collaboration with competition can be highly useful. But
  sometimes, it helps to collaborate with true outsiders: those
  who may be far-removed from your problem. Collaborating

with these sorts of outsiders may bring unique guidance and perspective that would not otherwise be considered.

IDEO, an award-winning design firm on the leading edge of innovation and creativity, regularly brings in true outsiders for collaboration through "Unfocus groups." Unfocus groups are composed of outsiders who are brought in to help refine and develop new products. A recent Unfocus group about shoes included a lounge singer, a mom, and a man who walks on fire and loves sandals. Each member of the group loved shoes, but their tastes were quite unique. When gathered together, they discussed their feelings toward footwear and shared their favorite shoes. They then developed prototypes for new shoes in small groups, helping those at IDEO gain a better sense for what people value in a shoe.[13]

Collaborating with outsiders may help you through difficult problems. Perhaps you could consult with former coworkers in your industry to help navigate through a new challenge. Or maybe you seek advice from outsiders to help you develop new ways to market your business. But bringing in an outsider's opinion makes sense: It could bring a new perspective and a fresh eye to enhance your ability to be successful and creative.

- **Encourage everyone to speak up, even the newbies and the typically quiet employees**
  Reserved individuals may be reluctant to offer ideas spontaneously in a large group. Thus, it is important to create other mechanisms to solicit input from these individuals. Opportunities to collaborate in writing or one-on-one with a new and/or reserved employee may be best.

  As well, leaders need to express the value of collaboration openly to employees and encourage them to challenge the status quo. At Pixar, the CEO tries to help new hires have confidence to speak up by talking "about the mistakes we've made and the lessons we've learned." He says, "My intent is to persuade them that we haven't gotten it all figured out and that we want everyone to question why we're doing something that doesn't seem to make sense to them."[14]

- **Make time for collaboration**
  In order to have successful collaboration, leaders must create opportunities for employees to engage with each other. Collaboration should be encouraged through regular feedback sessions and meetings that aim to advance the creation. Status meetings do not work, but collaborative work sessions do.

  In collaborative work sessions, participants give thoughtful feedback and strive to improve the overall uniqueness and success of the work. The sessions occur on a consistent basis and can take place in a conference room or shared workspace, or as a walking meeting outdoors. But the sessions should be active, with every participant speaking his/her opinions out of a desire to enhance the project

  Pixar conducts collaborative work sessions on a daily basis. In these sessions, egos are left behind, and daily work sharing is offered with one aim in mind: to create an excellent film. In these daily meetings, animators show incomplete work to the whole animation crew for feedback and input. Showing work in this incomplete fashion to the crew is vulnerable, but also crucial to the success of the overall film. The input enhances the work, and the team knows what is expected of them because the director (leader) shares feedback openly with everyone.[15]

- **Create a space that enhances collaboration**
  Collaboration needs not just time, but also space. Comfortable rooms and spaces to congregate aid in collaboration and should be considered when trying to enhance creativity in an organization. We believe this is such an important part of creativity that we have devoted an entire chapter to it (Chapter 7).

- **Reward collaboration**

  When you reward only individual performance, you will find that people want to work independently, for they will want individual credit and recognition for success. Sometimes, the employees will hide information for fear of others taking it. Other times, they will take credit for a creation that was not their own and inhibit future teamwork.

  Strong creative leaders recognize the value of collaboration and reward it accordingly. Teams are given bonuses, rather than just individuals. Groups are praised for project success, rather than standout team members. And each individual knows they bring unique and necessary value to the overall success of the collaboration: All are needed, yet none is more important than the other.

  As a leader, when you reward collaboration, individuals know that success comes not by withholding information, but by sharing it. The quiet but brilliant thinker is rewarded the same as the charismatic speaker. The analytical mind is valued as much as the artistic. All are rewarded for the group effort collaboratively, and all play a crucial role in the success of the work.

- **Conduct collaborative and individual reviews of employees**

  Every team should be reviewed for their ability to work together, generate ideas, and execute. Team reviews should be done to appreciate successes and improve the team. Leaders should explore listening skills, input, and tolerance for failure in these team reviews. The goal is to enhance collaboration, not berate individual members or reward standout individuals.

  Leaders should also conduct individual reviews to assess each person's strengths and weaknesses. As a strong leader, you will assess the individual's collaborative skills in these performance reviews and work with them to enhance the overall team and organization, rather than just the employee.

Try It Yourself

As a leader, reflect on the ideas below in writing. Take 15 minutes to answer the questions below, and evaluate how well you currently create opportunities for followers to collaborate.

- Are you an active member of an organization or association, and do you encourage your followers to belong to some as well?
- Do you seek advice from a broad range of individuals within and outside your organization? Do you encourage your followers to do that?
- Do you bring in groups and experts to share best practices and ideas?
- Are you overly protective of your work and creations, or do you regularly share it with others?
- Do you hold collaboration meetings aimed at improving the work and getting outsiders' perspectives?
- Do you offer feedback on team performance and your employee's ability to work collaboratively?
- Do you reward collaboration and teamwork, or just individual work?
- Are you certain that everyone has a voice in meetings and work sessions? Are you doing enough to help the new and reserved employees feel safe and comfortable sharing their ideas?

Next, choose two of those concepts above that you feel need improvement. Develop an action plan to enhance collaboration by working on those concepts. Can you give feedback in a more meaningful way, targeting collaboration skills, in your next one-on-one? Can you reward collaboration differently when you increase salaries next month? Or could you bring in outsiders to share best practices next quarter?

Put two things on your to-do list related to collaboration that you can accomplish by the end of the quarter. Slowly, but surely, you will build a more collaborative and creative organization.

Evaluating Your Teams: A Model for Collaboration

An Ideal Collaboration: Group Flow

Teams working together to create novel and unique solutions can falter or soar. Sometimes, the collaboration will include diverse participants and outsiders. Other times, we collaborate with those in our organization. In order to maximize that collaboration, Keith Sawyer, a leading scholar and author on creativity, suggests that participants work to achieve group flow. "Group flow" happens when a group performs at maximum effectiveness[16].

In order to achieve group flow, there must be:

1. **A Match Between the Group and the Goal**: Groups must have a collective goal, and the goal should match the group dynamics. Sometimes, the goal will be clear and well defined. In that case, the group should have a high level of structure. When there is an ambiguous goal for the group, less structure and more diversity is needed.

2. **Close Listening**: When group flow is achieved, participants listen with curiosity to other members of the group. They set aside their own agendas and offer unplanned responses in a free and open manner.

3. **Complete Concentration**: The group must be completely focused on the task. Distractions and multitasking are eliminated during group flow.

4. **Control and Autonomy**: The group is free to make decisions and plans. It is not overly bound by hierarchy.

5. **Blending Egos**: The group does not thrive because of one superstar. Rather, everyone offers unique contributions, and shared ideas emerge by building off each other's ideas.

6. **Equal Participation**: In group flow, everyone participates equally. Often, this means that people have some shared level of expertise, and everyone has respect for others.

7. **Familiarity**: In group flow, the members know each other and share some common knowledge and behaviors. However, they are not overly familiar with participants and thus often experience new insights in the group.

8. **Communication**: Group members constantly talk and share knowledge.

9. **Keep It Moving Forward**: Each person builds on ideas presented by others.
10. **The Potential for Failure**: Group members know there is a potential for failure and see it is an almost necessary step toward success.

Try It Yourself

Try to find or create a group where you can experience group flow.

1. Put together a team of people with similar levels of experience and expertise.
2. Make sure the team members know each other and the organization, but do not work together on a regular, daily basis. Be sure they can still surprise each other.
3. Create a meaningful collective goal for the group and give them autonomy to work and redefine the goals.
4. Make sure the group can make decisions and take action. Flow cannot be achieved if participants second-guess their ability to execute.
5. Listen closely and with curiosity to each person's input. Do not push your own agenda … stay open and curious.
6. Be sure that all members participate equally in the discussion.
7. Do not let one person be a superstar. This must be a collaborative effort.
8. Remove distractions and focus on your group task with total attention and concentration. It may help to meet in a neutral, open space to remove distractions.
9. Try to build off of the ideas you hear in an unplanned, unstructured way. Encourage group members to do the same.
10. Communicate about the project regularly and often. Keep the discussion active and open at all times.
11. Remember that it is okay and sometimes necessary to fail. Bad ideas lead to good ones.

Group flow is ideal for the employee, leader, and organization. The insight, knowledge sharing, and group work enhance the number of creative ideas. The mood is energetic and almost electric: Group members love working in this environment. Insights occur through passion and collaboration, and employees feel more alive overall. This brings creative success to the employees, yourself, and your organization.

Collaboration takes effort, time, and energy. In our fast-paced world, we look for quick answers and seek diverse feedback less and less. Time spent networking is, to some, time spent away from urgent work matters.

Yet networking, collaborating, and seeking feedback are part of the important work of creativity. In order to be truly creative and successful, we must seek outside opinions and feedback. Doing so will not only enhance our product or service offering, it will also enhance us as individuals and leaders. For through collaboration, we are able to gain new perspectives that may shift us and help us become a more effective, engaged individual in the workplace and overall.

Reflection Questions

1. Are you open to collaborating with others, or do you close yourself off and regularly work alone?
2. How might collaboration help you and your business?
3. Do you give your employees time to network and collaborate? Do you encourage this collaboration?
4. What may happen if you spent 5 percent of your time collaborating with a wide range of individuals to get new perspectives and feedback on your product and/or service offering?
5. Who could bring an outsider's perspective to your project? Can you ask this person for feedback? How might this person provide useful information to you and your work?
6. How can you improve your teams and create a more cooperative, collaborative environment overall? (For help, see Try It Yourself and Group Flow sections above.)

Notes

1. Sawyer, *Explaining Creativity the Science of Human Innovation*

2. "Creativity 50 2014: Michael Engleman." Advertising Age Creativity 50 RSS.

3. "Jean-Michel Basquiat: Now's the Time' on View at the Guggenheim Museum Bilbao."

4. Bockris, Victor. *Warhol the Biography*. Cambridge, UK: Da Capo Press, 2009.

5. Sawyer, *Explaining Creativity the Science of Human Innovation*.

6. Floyd Henry Allport. "The Influence of the Group Upon Association and Thought." *Journal of Experimental Psychology*, 3, 1920: 159–182.

7. Pisano, Gary P. "Which Kind of Collaboration Is Right for You?" *Strategic Direction*. 2009.

8. Groups perform better when an environment of trust exist where members can provide feedback or criticism in a way that does not diminish individual or group self-confidence. When social pressure or fear of rejection is high, willingness to engage within the group is often inhibited. Mumford, *Handbook of Organizational Creativity*.

9. Hunter, Mark Lee, and Herminia Ibarra. "How Leaders Create and Use Networks." *Harvard Business Review*.

10. Catmull, Edwin. "How Pixar Fosters Collective Creativity." *Harvard Business Review*. 2008.

11. Leigh, Buchanana. "Taking Teamwork to the Extreme." Inc.com. 2013. Accessed November 3, 2015; Sheridan, Richard. *Joy, Inc.: How We Built a Workplace People Love*. London, UK: Penguin Group, 2013.

12. "How Cross Functional Teams Contribute to a Stronger Alliance." Blog of Renault Nissan.

13. Kelley, Tom, and Jonathan Littman. *The Ten Faces of Innovation: IDEO's Strategies for Beating the Devil's Advocate & Driving Creativity throughout Your Organization; Tom Kelley; with Jonathan Littman*. London, UK: Profile Books, 2006.

14. Catmull, "How Pixar Fosters Collective Creativity."

15. Ibid.

16. Sawyer, *Explaining Creativity the Science of Human Innovation*.

CHAPTER 7

Creating Spaces to Enhance Engagement and Success

Over 50% of people in the workplace would rather be somewhere else; anywhere but here.[1]

Most people understand the effect that their home has on their life. If you walk around many communities in the United States, you'll find people working tirelessly on the weekends to mow their lawns, plant a beautiful garden, paint their homes, and beautify their surroundings. Yet, we spend between 8 and 12 hours a day in our work spaces and do little to make those environments more beautiful or comfortable.

In our offices, the layout and space are important. They send messages to employees, clients, and others about engagement, collaboration, and cohesion. Departments are often compartmentalized, and leaders are isolated in their own safe offices. Conference rooms are the only places for collaboration, sending a message that we prefer the status quo, even if others explicitly "say otherwise." And people are forced to remain in their offices, rather than work outside or in new environments. They have less time for vacation and travel, and simply are not able to rest their minds, explore new areas, or visit new cultures because they are working on "urgent" matters in the workplace.

These cold, isolated, and rather bare office spaces simply do not work. When we remove ourselves from nature, depersonalize our spaces, stare at white walls, and "collaborate" around a conference table, we accept the status quo and suffer. This sort of environment, where many Americans work, simply does not lend itself to successful creative outcomes. Compared with spaces that enhance nature, color, collaboration, and openness, our standard white-walled offices can lead to:

- Enhanced stress
- Diminished opportunity for collaboration
- A decreased ability to see new perspectives
- Less creative outcomes

We shape our buildings, and afterwards our buildings shape us.
—Winston Churchill

The right space has the potential to decrease stress and create a culture where people feel inspired to collaborate and develop new ideas. As architect Bob Fox said, "Space is a powerful tool. It brings together people, technology and ideas. It has the ability to communicate bold new concepts, and define the culture of an organization."[2] And creativity researcher Mihalyi Csíkszentmihályi agrees, stating, "The right milieu is important in more ways than one. It can affect production of novelty as well as its acceptance."[3]

In order to foster creativity, we need spaces to collaborate, incubate, and be inspired. Individuals who are stuck in the same space looking at the same walls will fail to thrive as creative leaders and beings.

In this chapter, we will explore the role that nature has in creativity, look at ways space can be designed to enhance creativity in an organization, and think about how collaboration, openness, places to incubate, and playful areas can be effective tools within our offices to enhance creativity.

The Role of Nature and Movement

When we are in nature, we often feel a greater sense of connection, purpose, and joy. Yet, we are spending less time in nature and more time staring at a screen. "Data suggests that children today spend only 15 to 25 minutes a day in outdoor play and sports and this number continues to decline. There has been a 20 percent decline in per capita visits to national parks since 1988, and an 18 to 25 percent decline in nature-based recreation since 1981."[4]

Ruth Ann Atcher and David L. Strayer recently conducted a study exploring the role of nature in creative problem solving and found that "four days of immersion in nature, and the corresponding disconnection from multi-media and technology, increases performance on a creativity, problem-solving task by a full 50%."[5] This result is not surprising because nature can help our mind rest and relax, giving us time to work through the creative process and problem solve.

Nature not only enhances creativity, but also enhances mood, playfulness and sometimes effectiveness.[6] Studies by Professors Andrea Faber Taylor and Francis Kuo show that nature and green areas enhance creative play in children and are preferred over manufactured playgrounds. And a study in Sweden shows that "asphalt playgrounds fostered interrupted play, whereas natural settings induce narratives with more depth and imagination."[7]

As well, we often walk, run, lift, and move when in nature, which enhances our ability to think differently. Exercising in nature can increase creativity, release our mind, and allow for ideas to emerge more spontaneously. When in nature, we sometimes collect our thoughts with greater ease and become more creative problem solvers.[8]

Several notable creatives found that nature and movement enhanced creativity. Freeman Dyson, physicist who is known for work in quantum electrodynamics, has said that his collegiate education was less about reading in the library than the "wide-ranging conversations he had with his tutor while strolling the paths around the college."[9] The long walks of poets Wordsworth, Coleridge, and Shelley were also linked to their creative output, while Virginia Woolf and Stephen King, "walked their books." Noted poet Mary Oliver has said, "I don't like buildings. I like motion."[10]

The problem is that we often sit by a computer, working in white-walled offices for 8 or even 10 hours a day. We rarely leave these offices and often find ourselves without a view to nature. It even seems that real plants are becoming less common in many office buildings today.

And yet it is so easy to move our work outside, at least sometimes. Laptops are the norm in American businesses and can be taken out for work on occasion. Conference calls can also be done outside, and walking meetings are becoming more commonplace as well.

It is also possible to bring nature inside, at least in part. Sometimes desks and tables can be turned to face the window and shades can be left open to allow for views of nature. Offices can be adorned with real plants, flowers, rocks, or even fountains with running water. In this way, a bit of nature will be brought in that may calm, soothe, and inspire employees.

Try It Yourself

Nature and movement provide excellent backdrops to inspire creativity. As a leader, try the following:

- Bring your laptop outside for an hour and do some work. Notice if you feel more effective in any way.
- Take 30 to 60 minutes in nature without electronics. Sit on a bench or rock, and contemplate a problem you need to solve or an area you want to improve at work. Don't write down anything … just sit in nature. Take notes when you return to the office.
- If possible, go for a walk or bike ride. Think about new and useful ways to solve a problem or enhance your work during this time, and take notes when you return.
- Try to hold one group meeting in the outdoors this week, and take some time to discuss new ways to enhance work during this meeting.

At the end of the week, reflect on the role nature played in enhancing your creativity as a leader. Build some time into future weeks to engage with nature in this way.

Travel and Creativity

The world is a book and those who do not travel read only a page.
—St. Augustine

Have you ever had a brilliant idea while on vacation? Or discovered a new way to solve an existing problem when wandering at a museum or enjoying a day at the beach?

Traveling to new and unusual places helps people see problems with a fresh eye and often inspires creative thinking. Creative individuals recognize that travel not only allows for incubation, but also can create new connections and ways of thinking that enhance effectiveness. Thus, it is important to give yourself and your employees opportunities to take time off, see new places, and experience fresh sights.

Former CEO of Citicorp, John Reed, believes in the power of travel, having had especially creative moments when he was away from the office on vacation. In two distinct instances while on vacation, Reed was able to brainstorm and write a lengthy letter to himself, spelling out the strengths, opportunities, and threats that Citicorp would be facing in the next several years. The first letter was written on a beach in the Caribbean, and the second, on a park bench in Florence. He found the travel gave him time and space to think clearly, stating, "In September before the third quarter, I had been kind of tired working Saturdays and Sundays, and I had gone to Italy for a week just to get away. I went to Rome for a couple of days, and then I went up to Florence. I'd get up early in the morning, and I'd wander around, and I sat on a park bench sort of between seven in the morning and noon, then in the afternoon I'd go visit museums and whatever. And I had a notebook, an Italian notebook, and I wrote myself long essays on what was going on and what I was worried about. And it helped me get my mind organized." These notebooks were spontaneous and unpremeditated. But without them, it is, "doubtful that Reed could have found a fresh perspective on the issues confronting his company, Citicorp."[11]

Many other creative works have been inspired while traveling. Hemingway wrote while in Cuba, Gauguin painted in Tahiti, and physics researcher Freeman Dyson cracked the problem of quantum electrodynamics—the theory of radiation and atoms—while riding on a Greyhound bus. Joanna Monteiro, winner of the Mobile Grand Prix at the Cannes Lions festival for creating Nivea's "Protection Ad," has said that to get out of a creative rut, you should "travel anywhere. You can't help coming back with a more open mind."[12]

Travel does bring one into a state of relaxation and open up the mind to different perspectives, cultures, and opportunities. Seeing how people live differently, exploring nature in new ways, and investigating the conversations of new communities can be great ways to open a person's mind to fresh ideas. Those new ideas could spark positive changes in your organization.

Sometimes, traveling to different locations helps individuals realize that there are many different, and valid, ways of living in the world. There isn't one right viewpoint; rather, there can be many ways to frame and solve a problem.

Traveling may have other benefits as well. Mary Helen Immordino-Yang, an associate professor of education and psychology at the University of Southern California, says that cross-cultural experiences have the potential to strengthen a person's sense of self. "What a lot of psychological research has shown now is that the ability to engage with people from different backgrounds than yourself, and the ability to get out of your own social comfort zone, is helping you to build a strong and acculturated sense of your own self," she says. "Our ability to differentiate our own beliefs and values … is tied up in the richness of the cultural experiences that we have had."[13]

Try It Yourself

Grab a notebook and pen, and head somewhere new for the day, weekend, or week. Pick a city you have never explored, and then:

- Sit in a restaurant or coffee shop and talk to the server. Investigate her story even if you do so silently: Where do you think she is from? What does she do for enjoyment? Do you think she has a family? Do you suspect she has traveled before?
- Walk around the city and imagine what it would be like to live there. How would your life be different?
- Sit on a bench in nature if possible and just watch the world go by. Here, you might think about a problem your organization is facing or a follower you hope to engage in new ways.
- Jot down some notes about your expedition and consider planning a monthly "trip" away from the office.

While taking a vacation may be taking hours away from the to-do list, it also gives an individual time to be reenergized, gain new perspectives, learn how to reframe things, and just relax the mind, allowing for creativity to blossom. These changes are paramount for creativity, problem solving, and leadership.

It may seem impractical to take time for travel. But sometimes, mini-trips can be just as effective. "If a plane ticket isn't an option, maybe try taking the subway to a new neighborhood. Sometimes, the research suggests, all that's needed for a creative boost is a fresh cultural scene."[14]

Indoor Spaces: Malleable, Stimulating, Reflective, Collaborative, Playful, and Personal (MSRCPP)

Make sure that where you work and live reflects your needs and your tastes. There should be room for immersion in concentrated activity and for stimulating novelty.[15]

More and more, companies and organizations are transforming spaces in order to enhance effectiveness, creativity, and output. When thinking about how to transform an office space, furniture design and configuration, lighting, color, and decorations should all be kept in mind. It is important to try to create places where people can collaborate, incubate, and play.

Google is known for its creative, open, collaborative, and fun work spaces. Clean air and natural light are priorities, with enhanced filtration systems and glass cubes that allow for natural light to flow into the interior of the building. There are open, comfortable areas to gather and collaborate. As well, whiteboards are scattered throughout Google spaces, sending a message that "shared thinking" is valued and ideas can happen anywhere, even in coffee lounges or hallways. Games and slides can be found in the vicinity, since Google encourages play. And there are no-tech spaces for incubation, including a water lounge in Zurich where Googlers can rest on a chaise lounge or massage chair. In these incubation spaces, employees must leave their phones at the door and remain quiet.[16]

Most companies, however, do not have Google's budget. Luckily, it does not take a big budget to make effective changes in a work environment. Changing a culture happens "with small tweaks … not big dramatic transformations,"[17] says Elliott Felix, founder of Brightfox, a strategy firm that helps organizations rethink space. Felix encourages leaders to think about the following:

- Where do people spend most of their time?
- Where do the best meetings happen?

- Where do people prefer to take phone calls?
- When is the office most full and noisy?
- When is it quiet?

Felix then urges leaders to talk to employees about space and culture and make changes in small ways. Some organizations find that putting puzzles and cards in a break room can do a lot to enhance relationships and build new alliances in an organization. Others test new office configurations by purchasing a larger table or adding a relaxation/tech-free space.

Try It Yourself

The Book, *Change Your Space, Change Your Culture,* details some key ideas to help leaders build strong cultures in their organizations. The authors suggest the following as a starting point for changing space and culture:

- Take a group of people into a large open room and give them sheets of paper, sticky notes, markers, and tape.
- Ask them to create a concept for a work environment (don't say "office"), using the following words: high energy, collaborative, healthy, productive, engaging, innovative, interactive, and "creative."
- Then, ask them to create a poster to describe what the experience is like in that environment.
- Finally, share the posters aloud, and ask, "Does this look or sound like your office?"
- See if there is a disconnect between their current office and the type of office they portray on their posters.
- Discuss the disconnect and talk about areas for change.

Think about three priorities that can easily be implemented to bridge the gap and make the office environment even a little bit more creative and engaging than it is now.

Malleable Spaces

At some of the most innovative companies, the staff is given freedom when it comes to space. They are able to move desks, chairs, tables, and work stations to enhance collaboration, effectiveness, and creativity.

At Oticon, a mid-size Danish manufacturer of hearing aids, workers are able to move items around in order to change the office layout.[18] Desks and filing cabinets are not fixed and can be pushed and reconfigured in new ways. This malleability creates flexibility, enhancing collaboration and inspiration.

Oticon is not alone. Many companies find that being able to move desks, chairs, filing cabinets, and tables enables them to work with a diverse group of individuals, collaborating based on energy, excitement, enthusiasm, passion, and talent. When the chairs, desks, and tables are movable, it can serve as a source of inspiration and motivation.[19] Indeed, when space can be broken down, changed, or reconfigured at a moment's notice, creativity is enhanced.

We are, after all, not just a brain but a body. If we remove desks and give people permission to assume different postures, they may enter a more relaxed, natural state that promotes engagement and creativity. "Students are good examples: they lie on the floor, perch on the backs of couches, bounce on their toes, and pace around the room … all during 'work' sessions." Such movement is healthy and can enhance communication and energy through body language, which ultimately may help people think differently and develop creative ideas.[20]

Unfortunately, we expect our employees to work at the same desk in the same cubicle for years. But this can change.

Won't the energy and inspiration in your office be different if employees could actually move their workspace for a week to engage and collaborate with different employees? Or if they could push their desk to a new area of the building and simply see a new perspective and hear different voices while working? But changing desks is workable and can be highly effective.

Stimulating Environments

Moveable work stations are one way to enhance creativity. But small changes can also be made to create a more stimulating environment. Exposing employees to a variety of stimuli on the walls and ceilings can encourage creative, divergent thinking.

For instance, Virgin has bold statements and graphics that express the creativity of the brand on their walls. Urban Outfitters' offices contain exposed ducts as well as vibrant patterns, textures, and colors. These images spark imagination and playfulness, and enhance the overall creative culture.

Color is another important component to creative space. Studies have shown that the color red helps people be more detail-oriented while blue boosts creativity.[21] Thus, it may be prudent to consider incorporating some blue into your workspace.

Beautiful and Personal

Poet and codirector of The Artists Way Creativity Camp James Navé believes that anyone can become a creative. But to do that, he says, we have to "create a space where we can feel intimacy" with ourselves and one another.[22]

Our spaces to work, including our office space, should be beautiful, if possible. "An attractive space can spark innovation strategies, and signal to employees that creativity is expected."[23] Some people enhance the beauty by bringing in more natural lighting and removing fluorescent lights, which can be agitating and diminish productivity. Others bring plants and nature inside to enhance beauty. And some just bring personal mementos and artifacts that inspire relaxation, passion, or purpose.

Walt Disney encourages personalized workspaces in this way. At Disney, employees bring in trophies, tokens, and collectibles that create a story about who they are and what motivates them. Some create workspaces that look like a jungle retreat. Others fill them with statues, trophies, stuffed animals, and plants. But in the end, these personalized spaces enhance their opportunity to be creative, authentic, and engaged.[24]

Places to Reflect

Hiding places offer a crucial respite from an open, collaborative environment ... If your space lacks one, people will go elsewhere to find it.[25]

—Kevin Kelly

Reflective hiding spaces allow the brain to rest and create opportunities for incubation. Google, Proctor & Gamble, Bloomberg, and DreamWorks Animation believe in the power of rest and create spaces at work to honor this value. Proctor & Gamble provides employees with nap pods, and the others have colorful fish tanks and zigzag pathways where employees can reflect, rest, and recharge. In these spaces, employees find that they can more readily contemplate next steps and creative new offerings.

In order to create a space to reflect, authors Scott Doorley and Scott Wittoft[26] recommend the following:

- First, choose a metaphor for a relaxation room: spa, yoga space, bedroom, garden, etc.
- Next, identify some of the key elements that make this space relaxing. Is it the lighting, music, soft pillows, or scent?
- Finally, use this list as inspiration to create your own "hiding place" with available resources or inexpensive purchases like lamps, candles, and pillows.

Try It Yourself

Investigate how you can make small changes to your space to enhance collaboration and creativity.

- Pull out the conference table for one week, and try to have all your meetings without the table. See how the meetings feel, and determine whether there is greater engagement and collaboration in the room.
- Bring everyone outside for your weekly meeting, or better yet, have the meeting while walking. Perhaps you start the meeting in one central location and have small groups brainstorm while taking a walk.
- Remove a few desks for a month and rent some moveable desks and stools instead. Perhaps requiring employees to move around will enhance energy, collaboration, and productivity.
- Transform an open office into a "no-tech hiding place with pillows and soft music."
- Hang some bulletin or white boards in the corridors and lunch spaces so people can randomly share their ideas, insights, and successes with others in the organization.
- Add some puzzles or games in the break or conference room to enhance playful collaboration.
- Ask every employee to bring in three personalized items for their office that inspires them in some way.

Collaborative and Playful Spaces

Creative meeting spaces do more than just gather people at a table. They bring people together, providing opportunities to organically relate and play on a variety of levels with a wide range of people. Sometimes adding a puzzle to the lunchroom or pulling out a conference room table and replacing it with comfortable chairs, couches, plants, and games can do the trick.

In the book *Make Space: How to Set the Stage for Creative Collaboration*, Doorley and Wittoft[27] recommend creating a small, blank "white room" aimed at helping people develop ideas in a collaborative manner. The white room should contain stools to promote upright posture, as well as a few chairs. Floor to ceiling dry erase surfaces should be on two or more adjacent walls because the space is meant to be an active place where team members create ideas with energy and vitality.[28] White focuses team members on the tasks, with ideas becoming the only color that fill the space. By keeping the space white, small, and open, team members work together with energy and focus that often cannot be replicated in a typical conference room.

Along with spaces to collaborate, there should be places and opportunities for play. DreamWorks Animation has a real basketball court outside, but others simply add a 20-dollar hoop over an office door. Still others keep nerf guns at the reception desk or shooters in the conference rooms. Sometimes, small tokens of playfulness in this way signal much more—that your company values and respects play, joy, and creativity.

Tom Gimbel is the founder and CEO of LaSalle Network and was recently named one of the top ten up and coming leaders to watch by *Entrepreneur Magazine*. Tom values playfulness and uses his existing intercom system to sing out messages to his employees on a regular basis. This playful attitude permeates the space and lets employees know that they too can be playful at work, without costing the company a dime.

Try It Yourself

Here, we will work on creating a more playful space at work.

- Bring in a puzzle and hand out a piece of that puzzle to each person on the team. Start the puzzle in a shared room (i.e., breakroom), and ask employees to complete the puzzle together throughout the month.
- Give every person in the office a $10 budget and ask them to buy something playful that they think would enhance the office space and/or culture. Employees can purchase posters, games, toys, etc.
- Share the trinkets in a group meeting and place them around the office to encourage play.

Our spaces influence us in many ways. They can help us feel engaged, or diminish our motivation altogether. We know that our heavy wooden desks and uninspired offices do not work. So take the time to make small changes to your office space, and watch the transformation begin.

Reflection Questions

1. What does your office space say about your organizational culture?
2. How can you spend more of your working time in nature? How can you bring more nature into your office?
3. How often do you visit new places and explore unique cultures? How might this sort of "travel" enhance your work and life? How can you encourage your employees to explore new sights as well?
4. How can you enhance your office space to make it more suitable for collaboration? Can you add whiteboards to the lunch area? Or perhaps you can introduce games into that space to enhance relationships across groups.
5. How can you make part of your space more stimulating? Can you add color to the walls? Or stimulating artwork?
6. What does your office say about you? How can you make your space more personalized and create a story about yourself in the office? How can you encourage your followers to do the same?

Notes

1. Miller, Rex, and Mabel Casey. *Change Your Space, Change Your Culture How Engaging Workspaces Lead to Transformation and Growth.* Hoboken, NJ: Wiley, 2014.

2. Ibid.

3. Csikszentmihalyi, *Creativity: Flow and the Psychology of Discovery and Invention.*

4. Atchley, Ruth Ann, David L. Strayer, Paul Atchley, and Jan De Fockert. "Creativity in the Wild: Improving Creative Reasoning through Immersion in Natural Settings." PLoS ONE. p E51474.

5. Ibid.

6. Several recent studies have found that spending time in nature provides cognitive benefits. For instance, a group of teens who spent time walking in an arboretum were in much better moods and did better in short-term memory tests than another group of students who had just walked down a set of busy streets. Leader, Jessica. "Nature-Creativity Study Links The Great Outdoors With Positive Psychological Effects." The Huffington Post. May 31, 2012.

7. Barron and Barron. *The Creativity Cure: A Do-it-yourself Prescription for Happiness.*

8. Ibid.

9. Csikszentmihalyi, *Creativity: Flow and the Psychology of Discovery and Invention.*

10. "Mary Oliver - Listening to the World." On Being. www.onbeing.org/program/mary-oliver-listening-to-the-world/7267/audio?embed.=1

11. Csikszentmihalyi, *Creativity: Flow and the Psychology of Discovery and Invention.*

12. Penteado, Claudia. "Creativity 50 2014: Joanna Monteiro." Advertising Age Creativity 50 RSS. http://adage.com/article/creativity-50/creativity-50-2014-joanna-monteiro/296247/

13. Crane, Brent. "For a More Creative Brain, Travel." The Atlantic. March 31, 2015.

14. Ibid.

15. Csikszentmihalyi, *Creativity: Flow and the Psychology of Discovery and Invention*, 196.

16. Groves, Kursty, and Will Knight. *I Wish I Worked There!: A Look inside the Most Creative Spaces in Business.* Hoboken: Wiley, 2010.

17. Segren, Elizabeth. "Designing A Happier Office On The Super Cheap." Fast Company. March 30, 2015.

18. That's Ewing, 2007, Cited in Kaufman, *The Cambridge Handbook of Creativity.*

19. Udo-Ernst Haner, 2005, Spaces for Creativity and Innovation in Two Established Organizations, Creativity and Innovation Management, 14(3), pp.288–298

20. Doorley, Scott, and Scott Witthoft. *Make Space: How to Set the Stage for Creative Collaboration.* New Jersey: John Wiley & Sons, 2011.

21. Mehta, R, Zhu, R. (Feb 2009). Blue or Red? Exploring the Effect of Color on Cognitive Task Performances. *Science* 27: Vol. 323, Issue 5918, pp. 1226–1229

22. "Exploring Creativity with Poet/Creative James Navé." www.archinia .com/blogs/228-exploring-creativity-with-poetcreative-james-nave .html

23. Kaufman, *The Cambridge Handbook of Creativity.* 158.

24. Groves and Knight, *I Wish I Worked There!: A Look inside the Most Creative Spaces in Business.* 246.

25. Doorley and Witthoft, *Make Space: How to Set the Stage for Creative Collaboration.*

26. Ibid.

27. Ibid.

28. Showerboard is the cheapest option and can be purchased for as little as $20 a board.

CHAPTER 8

Creativity and Leadership Training that Inspires Positive Growth

Leadership Development

Leadership development is a hot topic. U.S. companies spend almost 14 billion dollars annually on leadership development programs, and executives consistently rank it as a top priority for their organizations.[1] We are regularly investigating the best tools, methods, and techniques to develop our leaders and have discovered some key ideas that work.

Experience, education, assessment, challenge, and support are key components for successful development.[2] Effective training programs include elements of experiential training like challenging case studies, role-plays, and/or work assignments. They also include education on leadership concepts, together with assessment, support, and feedback. This combination of lecture, experience, simulation, role-play, and reflection helps leaders learn new skills, practice them, and reflect on their successes and failures. It also enriches the experience for learners by engaging them in a variety of ways.

Strong development programs need to do more than engage the leader. Hopefully, a person comes out of a development experience having achieved new skills and experience to propel them forward. Thus, clear learning and growth objectives related to the leaders' development are crucial in a training program, and should be communicated to the group. In this way, participants will know what they will be learning and why. They then are given time to practice and use the new skills during training and afterward. They are also assessed on these new skills and given regular feedback on progress. This combination helps solidify the training to grow leadership capacity.[3] Sometimes, this sort of program lasts a few hours, and sometimes it continues for several months.

The Center for Creative Leadership (CCL) offers a number of programs that successfully combine knowledge, practice, experience, and reflection as we have discussed. The CCL's Leadership Development Program for managers (LDP) is ranked as one of the best leadership development programs in the world. It offers three comprehensive stages that have been shown to help participants have a greater impact on their organizations. In stage 1, Prepare, participants engage in an assessment of their own leadership skills where they analyze their current behaviors, preferences, competencies, and developmental needs. In stage 2, Engage, participants partake in experiential activities and skill-building exercises, including a mock business environment for practice. The Engage section also includes time for feedback and reflection, with a half-day, personal session led by a certified CCL coach and peer learning groups. Finally, in stage 3, Apply, participants continue their learning through ongoing phone coaching sessions, an assessment to measure progress, and access to eLearning designed to reinforce lessons from the program.[4]

Try It Yourself

Let's evaluate the type of leadership development training you have been doing in your organization and/or for yourself. Do your trainings offer:

1. Assessment to determine current strengths, weaknesses, and needs of the participants?
2. Clear learning objectives and goals that can be measured to determine effectiveness?
3. An educational component that shares a proven theory or technique solidly backed by research? Or do you teach material without evidence that the concepts actually work?
4. Role-play and/or simulations that give participants opportunities to apply the new knowledge?
5. Opportunities to use the information/training in real-work experiences?
6. Coaching and feedback on current behaviors and skills?

7. Coaching and feedback on areas for growth, together with continued coaching and feedback on the participant's implementation of the training materials?
8. Opportunities for personal reflection?
9. Continued assessments to measure growth and areas for improvement even after the training?
10. Continued access to information and resources to help participants dig deeper into the concepts?

If your trainings lack some of these key attributes, then work to implement them into your programs one-by-one. Small enhancements can greatly improve development programs and create strong leaders in your organizations.

Creativity Development

Like leadership, creativity can be taught and developed. It is not a characteristic that is fixed at birth, nor is it reserved for a few gifted people. Rather, it is a common characteristic of all human beings that can be developed and cultivated.[5] And, since we want more creative leaders, it is prudent to consider adopting some form of creativity training in our organizations.

Ellis Paul Torrance, a leading scholar on creativity and creator of the Torrance Test of Creative Thinking, identified 142 studies that showed creativity training does enhance performance.*[6] More recent analysis of over 70 studies also supports this view by again proving that creativity training enhances performance. Informally, some of the most creative people in business cite the importance of being open to new experiences and unfamiliar ways of thinking. They too believe that creativity can be taught through training.[7]

Wharton Business School marketing professor Jerry (Yoram) Wind teaches creativity courses at Wharton and says that "in any population,

---

*Much of the research shows that training can enhance success during the ideation stage of creativity, resulting in more and better ideas.

basically the distribution of creativity follows the normal curve. At the absolute extreme you have Einstein and Picasso, and you don't have to teach them—they are the geniuses. Nearly everyone else in the distribution, and the type of people you would deal with at leading universities and companies, can learn creativity."[8]

Creativity Training in Organizations: The IBM Program

Creative thinking programs are now relatively commonplace in businesses and organizations. In 1956, Louis R. Mobley realized that IBM's success depended on teaching executives to think creatively. As a result, the IBM Executive School was built around six insights that include the following:

1. **Traditional teaching methodologies like reading, lecturing, testing, and memorization are counterproductive.** Nonlinear thinking is key to creativity.

    At the IBM training, executives work through case simulations and puzzles during training. The "right" answers are not clear, and lectures and talks are not given. Rather, participants work through ambiguous, difficult problems together, sharing ideas and learning how to think like a creative person again.

2. **Becoming creative is an *unlearning* rather than a *learning* process.** Participants work out of their comfort zones and try to upend existing assumptions.

3. **Creativity takes time, and training does as well.** Executives work through a 12-week boot camp, filled with brain teasers and experiments in alternative modes of thinking.

4. **To be creative, you must immerse yourself with creative people, sometimes in an unstructured way.** The IBM Executive School was often unstructured, with many of the benefits accruing through informal peer-to-peer interaction.

5. **Creativity is highly correlated with self-knowledge**, and so it is important to understand yourself and your personal bias.

6. **Creatives know that it is important to make mistakes and be wrong.** The school gave students permission to be wrong.

The IBM program successfully enhanced creativity in the organization and provided key touchstones that may be important to consider with creativity training in other businesses. In general, the most effective creativity training programs are longer in duration and focus on cognitive skills. They are not conducted in a singular, intensive course, nor are they lecture based. As well, these courses include realistic and relevant exercises and case studies.

Creativity Training Programs in Educational Institutions

Many formal creativity training programs are conducted in educational institutions. The Productive Thinking Program, Myers-Torrance Workbooks, CoRT Thinking Lessons, and Purdue Creative Thinking Program are some of the most commonly used creativity enhancement training programs in educational contexts. The Productive Thinking Program (Covington et al.) teaches a variety of ways to manage and monitor one's thinking through a self-paced set of 16 detective stories that encourage children to reframe problems and generate ideas.[9] The Myers–Torrance Workbook (Myers and Torrance, 1964, 1965, 1966, 1968) is also a written program, aimed at enhancing cognitive abilities that are important in creativity. Finally, the Purdue Creative Thinking Program is a set of 32, 15-minute audio-taped lessons, with each one focused on a famous creator in history.

The CoRT Thinking Lessons were developed by Edward DeBono in the 1960s and widely used throughout the United States, in the United Kingdom, Ireland, Canada, Australia, New Zealand, Israel, and Malta. CoRT is a 60-lesson course aimed at helping students organize their thinking, broaden their perceptions, observe how arguments are presented, and discover ways to change concepts and patterns in thinking. The program has been called the Spectacle Method because it helps participants see the world more broadly.[10] For instance, the first lesson, the PMI, asks students to look to a positive direction, then a negative direction, and finally an "interesting" direction. By doing this, they scan across a scene and look for new ways to explore a problem. PMI helps eliminate the immediate acceptance or rejection of an idea, leading to more creative options.

The CoRT Thinking Lessons help students develop lateral thinking: a generative way of thinking that can break away from assumptions and allow exploration of relationships in new ways. It has been used primarily in educational institutions, but can be used and/or adapted more broadly as well.

Creative Problem Solving Method

The creative problem solving (CPS) method is widely used in educational institutions and business organizations. This method helps people redefine problems and develop innovative solutions in a step-by-step process that has been proven to lead to a higher frequency of ideas. CPS begins with two assumptions:

- Everyone is creative.
- Creativity can be learned and enhanced.

The most recent iteration of the CPS method has four stages—clarifying, ideating, developing, and implementing. Within each stage, participants use divergent and convergent thinking. **Clarifying** is ensuring you're asking the right question. Here, participants identify the goal or challenge, gather data to enable clear understanding of the challenge, and create questions that invite solutions. In the second stage, **ideate**, participants explore ideas that answer the challenging questions. The third stage, **develop**, has participants working to find solutions by evaluating, strengthening, and selecting those that seem like a good option. Finally, in the **implement** stage, participants create a plan of action.[11]

CPS balances divergent and convergent thinking. Divergent thinking generates a lot of ideas and options, while convergent thinking evaluates those ideas and results in a decision. In CPS, divergent thinking and convergent thinking are separate, with participants generating lots of ideas before evaluating them.

When developing ideas (divergent thinking) for CPS, participants should do the following:

- **Defer judgment.** In ideation, participants should not evaluate ideas. Doing so limits the number of ideas and prevents out-of-the-box thinking.

- **Combine and build.** Here, participants use one idea as a springboard for another. For instance, someone may suggest using an artist from a local college to develop new images for marketing. Participants could then build on the idea of hiring artistic individuals and suggest hiring a storyteller, clay artist, and so on. Each of those suggestions will help create new ways of thinking about marketing. And while none may ultimately work, the combine and build method brings more novel ideas to the table.
- **Seek wild ideas.** Wild ideas lead to novel ideas, and if we want to expand creativity, we need to stretch ourselves and think outside the box.
- **Go for quantity.** When working on divergent thinking, participants should try to create a number of ideas and not stop at the first good one. The Creative Education Foundation recommends setting goals around quantity and encourages individuals to list 30 ideas in 7 minutes, with groups listing 50 ideas in 7 minutes.[12]

After generating a large number of ideas, participants should begin to evaluate those ideas. In this stage of convergent thinking, criteria are used to evaluate, refine, and improve options. Convergent thinking demands deliberate, careful thought. It should not be rushed, and every option should be considered fairly.[13] In this way, participants take time to do the following:

- **Improve existing ideas**. Here, participants ask "how can this idea be better" for each of those listed.
- **Consider what works in an idea** and judge with an eye toward improvement.
- **Consider the wild, novel ideas** and work to improve them.

The CPS method has been proven effective. It helps define problems, create additional options for resolution, and evaluate ideas in a more thoughtful way.[14] As well, the method has been proven successful with small groups, leading to enhanced involvement in the problem-solving process, less criticism of ideas, and a higher number of options.[15] The training is rather comprehensive and often taught at the annual Creative Problem Solving Conference, led by the Creative Education Foundation, each summer.

Nonetheless, parts of the CPS method can successfully be implemented into existing development and training programs, as shown below in the Try It Yourself activity.

Try It Yourself

The entire CPS method is complex and cannot be done as a "try it yourself" exercise. However, the evaluation matrix tool that is used to help analyze possible solutions can be used in a simple way. Doing so will enhance creative thinking in your employees. To use this method, do the following:

1. Define the problem that you want to solve.
2. Brainstorm a list of options to solve that problem. Remember to defer judgment, combine ideas, aim for wild ideas, and go for quantity.
3. Now, evaluate those ideas using the matrix description below.

To create the matrix, participants will first generate criteria to evaluate those solutions. Some criteria may include: "within our budget," "within our resources," "appeal to our customers," "ease of implementing," and so forth. Then, choose a few criteria that are most important for the project and put that criterion into "positive question form," allowing for a YES answer to give a positive response. Thus, rather than ask "will we lack resources for the idea," the question should be framed as "will we have enough resources for this idea." If you answer yes to "will we lack resources," you don't have a positive response to that idea. But a "yes" response to the question "will we have the resources" does generate a positive response to the idea overall.

Next, create a matrix with the key criteria heading various columns. It can look like this:

	Will we have resources for this?	Will this fit in our budget?	Will customers understand this concept?
Option 1			
Option 2			

Finally, develop a potential rating system to indicate how well each option satisfied the criteria. You could use a simple number scale (1–5), a thumbs-up/thumbs-down illustration, or something in between. The key is to keep it simple. You then run through the options and write in the rating on the matrix, making the best option(s) more clearly visible.

Evaluation Matrix

	Will we have resources for this?	Will this fit in our budget?	Will customers understand this concept?
Option 1	4	3	5
Option 2	2	5	4

This evaluation matrix can be used in almost any brainstorming session after ideas are offered. It is a useful tool to evaluate ideas and one that can be taught to expand creative thinking.

Miscellaneous Training Programs Aimed at Enhancing Leadership and Creativity

Cooking, Creativity, and Leadership Development

There are a number of other training programs beyond CPS that can enhance creativity. Even cooking can teach people to be more inventive and creative. When cooking, you may learn that controlled recipes work, or find that tweaking a recipe brings better results. Extravagance may be best in one instance, while simple dishes might be more appreciated in another. With cooking, there are always second chances, since you can turn something bad into something decent most of the time.

In the kitchen, chefs need to adapt, experiment, and play. They remain open to new ways of preparing dishes and coping with change. They may tweak recipes because they lack resources. These skills of adaptability, coping, experimenting, and play are paramount for strong, 21st-century leaders. Thus, some trainers are using cooking as a way to enhance creativity, highlight strengths, and improve teamwork.

Leadership Vision Consulting is one such organization. For them, workshops begin with an overview of Clifton's Strength Finder, where participants are told about the importance of leading from strengths and discuss how strength-based leadership works. Then, they cook a meal in small groups while the trainers observe team members. Throughout the cooking, trainers may comment on the participants' behaviors, stating things like "When the potatoes didn't turn out right, you seemed to be able to go with the flow and improvise pretty easily. Do you think your adaptability and positivity helped with that?"[16] This active learning enhances participants' understanding of their own strengths, as well as those of their peers.

LEGO® SERIOUS PLAY™

Like cooking, LEGO building can enhance creativity and strategic thinking. LEGO® SERIOUS PLAY™ was developed by Executive Discovery, a member of the LEGO Group. It grew out of the research and experience of a number of academics and practitioners searching for better ways to meet the demands of the business world.[17] In a LEGO® SERIOUS PLAY™ workshop, participants manipulate and play with LEGO bricks, using different parts of the brain and encouraging creative thinking. The use of the bricks often eliminates hierarchy issues and helps people work together more effectively.

Workshops often begin with participants creating models of their issue or problem out of LEGO. They are given opportunities to share these models with others, opening up conversation and dialogue about the differing perspectives on a problem. LEGO® SERIOUS PLAY™

participants use the bricks to answer questions, build ideas, and share stories. The 3D bricks help them see and explain things in a new way. The approach suggests that hands-on learning produces more meaningful understanding.

The Thunder Bay Regional Health Sciences Centre is an acute care facility serving the needs of people living in Northwestern Ontario. It has used LEGO® SERIOUS PLAY™ to help build teamwork within a new organizational structure, as well as for conflict management and senior leadership workshops. The Director of Communications believes that LEGO® SERIOUS PLAY™ has been instrumental to their success as a team, stating "progressive reconstruction of the pieces provided information about each other that otherwise would have been impossible to achieve in the short-term. It is an amazing transparent exercise that creates a deeper level awareness of senior team interdependence."[18, 19]

Try It Yourself

LEGO® SERIOUS PLAY™ facilitators are trained in the methods of LEGO, and enable deep connection and learning for participants. An experienced leadership facilitator will also solidify learnings in a cooking workshop. However, even without such facilitation, leaders can informally use LEGO and/or cooking as a way to enhance teamwork, encourage dialogue and create more playfulness and experimentation at work.

First, purchase or borrow LEGO bricks of various sizes and bring them to a meeting. The blocks do not need to belong to a set or include instructions.

Begin the meeting by dumping the LEGO on the table and giving participants a few minutes to play and get reacquainted with the toy. Next, ask participants to make a model of a problem you are currently facing. The problem could be about teamwork, collaboration, workload, or a business problem more directly related to a project. Once the models are complete, encourage all participants to share aloud. People should merely listen during the sharing time, and not comment on each other's models in any way. After all have shared the

(*Continued*)

models, participants can discuss their take-away and work to develop a solution.

To take it further, think about a skill that you might want to help your employees learn or develop. If you want them to experiment more, force them to take apart their design after sharing and build something completely different in less than 3 minutes. If you want them to work on collaboration, ask them to work in small groups to design a solution using LEGO. You could encourage discussion among the group or ask them to work together silently, helping them cultivate trust and understanding in a new way. Alternatively, if you want them to work on the creative process, you could ask them to plan for their LEGO creation, building in time to let their plans fester (incubation). After preparation and incubation, they could then build the LEGO model and get feedback (verification) from others.

In the end, LEGO can be used formally or informally to bring new ideas, enhance visual and 3D thinking, and improve any number of creativity and leadership skills. It is easy to add LEGO to your existing meetings, and can help create a culture of creativity and fun.

Arts-Based Training

The arts help individuals understand the creative process, and lead to greater self-knowledge. Research by the College Entrance Examination Board has shown that students engaged in fine arts score up to 63 points higher on verbal and 44 points higher on math exams on a common scale than students with no arts participation.[20] As well, those who participate in fine arts tend to exhibit some of the same characteristics that define leaders, including increased creativity, confidence, self-awareness and perseverance. Participation in theater helps people learn about communication and teamwork, both of which are leadership crucial skills.

In an effort to use fine arts to enhance training, companies now intertwine art, music and drama into their work. Some trainers use storytelling, dance, and art to enhance employees' creativity.

Get Storied is the leading school for business storytelling, serving over 250,000 clients each month. Through their trainings, they apply the power of story to innovation, strategy and leadership. Michael Margolis, founder of Get Storied, believes that storytelling is at the root of transformation, and helps organizations learn how to create compelling stories in a collaborative, flexible way. The training enhances the vision and strategies of an organization, and does so in a fluid way, enhancing creativity overall.[21]

Participants can enhance their skills and creativity using art through The Art Institute of Chicago and Catalyst Ranch's Art-Work program, which is a series of five one-day workshops. In these workshops, designed to develop professional skills through art observation, participants can focus on creativity, teambuilding, communication, diversity and/or leadership. The morning starts in the galleries of the Art Institute, where participants visually observe artwork and listen to each other's perspectives. Everyone's observations have validity, helping people appreciate different ways of perceiving and interpreting the world. In the afternoon, participants perform art-based activities in order to build trust, find shared values, and shift perceptions. This combination of observation and hands-on artwork activates both sides of the brain and helps participants explore their creative potential, develop collaborative skills and expand their thinking. It has been used successfully by several companies, including McGraw-Hill, who believes the arts-based training helped employees be more creative while confronting their assumptions in a nontraditional environment.[22]

Shakespeare's plays can also shed light on assumptions and provide powerful insight into key leadership skills. At the Guthrie Theater, Veteran actors therefore combine Shakespeare performances with trainee participation to explore how the plays highlight current challenges of leadership. The theater also teaches hands-on classes, helping participants become more engaging speakers and listeners.[23]

Music in Training

Music can also be an effective way to train leaders. If given the opportunity to conduct a musical piece, a person can see the importance of vision, flow, and collaboration. When presented with the chance to play a new instrument, participants are forced out of their comfort zones. And when forced to make music as a group, members must rely on each other for assistance and need to practice listening skills in a deeper way.

The City of London Sinfonia regularly uses music as a tool to train employees of business organizations. In the training, participants play or conduct, breaking out of their comfort zones, failing in front of each other, and supporting each other through that failure. Sometimes, they recognize that they are not in sync with their team musically or did not conduct the musicians with a shared vision. This insight helps them understand the power of a shared vision in a new way. "Working with people outside our normal activity, as with musicians, can bring out … learning in a non-threatening environment" (p. 43).[24]

Percussionist Gary Muszynski also uses music in teambuilding, creativity, and leadership development training. "As his participants jam on a Nigerian udu drum, marimbas and other percussion instruments … they learn to overcome their inhibitions and find where they fit in—musically and back at the workplace."[25]

Improvisation

Improvisation demands flexibility and tolerance for ambiguity and requires active, engaged listening and collaboration. Improvisation is a form of live theater in which the plot, characters, and dialogue of scene are made up in the moment. Often, audience members offer suggestions to help improvisers begin their story. From there, anything can happen. Some cardinal rules of improvisation are as follows:

- **Agree.** Do not block or deny someone's proposed story. If someone responds to an actor by saying no, the story almost always falls flat. The actors stop offering ideas for fear of hearing no, and simply have no room to develop the performance. In improv, when an actor says they are holding a unicorn, it is important to simply agree with that idea. The rule of agreement helps participants work from an open-minded place while respecting their partners in the process

  Wouldn't our leaders be more effective if they respected others' ideas and began from an open-minded place, like in improv?

- **Say "yes and," rather than "no."** In improv, participants must go with whatever the other actor brings to the story.

Then, they need to add onto that story to keep it moving forward. In this way, participants have a responsibility to contribute and add something to the discussion.

Wouldn't our work be more engaging if our leaders said "Yes, and …" rather than "no" a bit more often

- **Focus on the here and now**. In improv, you must immerse yourself in the here and now, or you will lose track of the story and not be able to continue. Improvisers cannot check their phones, think about their to-do lists, or multitask.

  Wouldn't our leaders be more inspiring and engaged if they focused on the here and now a bit more often, particularly when it comes to relationships?

- **Change!** Characters need to be in the moment, and let themselves to be influenced and affected by new revelations and experiences. They should change themselves, their locations, and/or their actions within a story on the basis of new revelations.

  Wouldn't our organizations be more successful if leaders more thoughtfully considered new occurrences in the workforce and world, and modified their leadership and/or organizations to adapt to those changes?

- **There are no mistakes … only opportunities**. Every contribution has value and can change a story for the better.[26]

  Wouldn't followers be more likely to share ideas if leaders believed that mistakes can lead to opportunities? And wouldn't that tolerance for "mistakes" lead to more creativity in the end?

The rules for improvisation also apply to leadership and are being used to train leaders more and more. Second City Works in Chicago has successfully trained hundreds of leaders using improv, claiming that "businesses that thrive in the chaos of ever-present change are the ones with a new toolkit. It's a toolkit that values speed, agility, collaboration, comfort with change, willingness to fail, and the creativity to solve old problems in new ways. Ultimately, they have the toolkit of an improviser."[27] At Second City Works training, leaders sometimes create new stories for their company's brand or begin to function more effectively as a team. But almost every time, they learn and use processes that can enhance their overall ability to be creative and lead in a more transformative, open-minded way.

Investing in Your People

Training programs are worthwhile. They take time, effort, and money. But they also enhance our leadership and creativity, leading to better results and engagement.

People want to grow, be challenged, and develop. They also want to be engaged. Using music, improv, arts, and/or theater in training can bring new insights, challenges, and ideas to develop our employees. CPS can be learned and practiced, and leadership programs can be tweaked to bring more engagement and learning.

As a leader, it is important to seek out training that will engage, motivate, inspire, and teach our employees. When you do that by incorporating the concepts in this chapter, your employees have more passion and loyalty toward their work. They will grow in some way and also feel that the organization supports them in this growth. The training will be inspiring and not just another "lecture" or "motivational pep talk."

Reflection Questions

1. Do you engage in regular training programs to advance your creativity and leadership?
2. Do you offer development opportunities for your followers to help them grow as leaders and creative employees?
3. How valuable is creativity and leadership to you? Are you investing enough into the development of these skills?
4. Are your current training programs meaningful? Do they offer education, experience, assessment, and feedback to help participants fully develop as leaders?

5. What creativity programs sound interesting to you: Cooking, LEGO building, arts-based work, or music? Would it be possible to attend one of these trainings in the next year?

6. How can you sprinkle creativity training into your workplace? Can you use LEGO in meetings, have employees create stories about your organization, or incorporate cooking or arts in some way?

Notes

1. Gurdjian, Pierre, Thomas Halbeisen, and Kevin Lane. "Why Leadership-development Programs Fail." McKinsey Quarterly. 2014.

2. Antonakis, John. *The Nature of Leadership*. Thousand Oaks, CA: Sage Publications, 2004. p 129.

3. Yukl, Gary A. *Leadership in Organizations*. 8th ed. Englewood Cliffs, NJ: Prentice-Hall, 2012.

4. "Leadership Development Program (LDP)." Center for Creative Leadership. www.ccl.org/leadership/pdf/programs/LDP.pdf

5. Sawyer, *Explaining Creativity the Science of Human Innovation,* Oxford, UK: Oxford University Press, 2006. p. 171.

6. Torrance, E.P. (1995). Why Fly? New Jersey: Ablex Publishing.

7. Nagy, Evie. "Can Creativity Be Taught? 73% of Creative People Say Yes." Fast Company. February 19, 2014.

8. "Can Creativity Be Taught?" Knowledge Wharton Can Creativity Be Taught. http://knowledge.wharton.upenn.edu/article/can-creativity-be-taught/

9. Entwistle, Noel. *Handbook of Educational Ideas and Practices (Routledge Revivals)*. Taylor and Francis, 2015. Sternberg, Robert J. *Handbook of Intelligence*. Cambridge, UK: Cambridge University Press, 2000. p. 528.

10. Maxwell, William. *Thinking, the Expanding Frontier: Proceedings of the International, Interdisciplinary Conference on Thinking Held at the University of the South Pacific*, January, 1982. Philadelphia, PA: Franklin Institute Press, 1983.

11. "Creative Problem Solving Resource Guide." Creative Education Foundation. 2014. www.creativeeducationfoundation.org/wp-content/uploads/2015/06/CPS-Guide-6-3-web.pdf

12. Ibid.

13. Ibid.

14. Puccio, Murdock, and Mance. "Creative Problem Solving for Organizations: A Focus on Thinking Skills and Styles." *Korean Journal of Thinking and Problem Solving*, 2005.

15. Ibid.

16. Freeburg, Nathan. "How We Use Cooking to See Strengths—Leadership Vision." Leadership Vision. February 25, 2014. www.leadershipvisionconsulting.com/how-we-use-cooking-to-see-strengths/

17. LEGO® SERIOUS PLAY™. "The Science of LEGO® SERIOUS PLAY™." www.strategicplay.ca/upload/documents/the-science-of-lego-serious-play.pdf

18. Strategic play. "Case Study: RBC (Royal Bank of Canada)." www.strategicplay.ca/upload/documents/lego-serious-play-rbc-.pdf

19. Hequet, Marc. "Creativity Training Gets Creative." *Training*. 1992.

20. *College-Bound Seniors National Report: Profile of SAT Program Test Takers*. Princeton: The College Entrance Examination Board, 2001.

21. "Get Storied—Our Curriculum." Get Storied. www.getstoried.com/our-curriculum/

22. Journal of Business Strategy. Special edition on arts-based learning for business. Oct 2005 Volume: 26 Issue: 5. Republished as Arts-based Learning for Business by Harvey Seifter and Ted Buswick (editors). See also. www.catalystranchmeetings.com/downloads/ArtWorkBrochure.pdf

23. www.guthrietheater.org/education/business_training

24. Creativity in leadership development. September 2009. training-journal.com

25. Hequet, "Creativity Training Gets Creative."

26. Leonard, K. and Yorton, T. (2015). Yes, And: How Improvisation Reverses "No, But" Thinking and Improves Creativity and Collaboration--lessons from the Second City. Harper Collins.

27. "The Second City—50 Years of Funny." www.secondcity.com/works/

CHAPTER 9

10 Immediate Shifts to Become a More Creative and Effective Leader

Many of us are looking for a prescription to follow that will enhance creativity. Unfortunately, there is not any one prescription. Rather, organizational creativity requires a combination of transformational leadership with the right culture, space, and opportunities to collaborate. People can be trained in a variety of ways to be more creative, lead better, and solve problems more effectively. But these methods will not work fully in isolation. Culture, collaboration, and strong overall leadership are still needed.

As we have seen, strong leaders need to make creativity the number one item on their agenda. They strive to be a role model, leading in a transformative way and working to build strong, positive cultures. They create spaces conducive to creativity and make collaboration crucial. Yet all of this takes a good deal of time and energy.

So how about a quick fix? Certainly, leaders can take small steps on a daily basis to enhance creativity in an organization while also paying attention to the larger goals and ideas we explored in earlier chapters. Sometimes, simply changing your language or meeting location begins the shift, and creates small wins to propel larger changes.

Thus, our final chapter is devoted to the present moment: What can a leader do to immediately enhance creativity? Below are ten items that require small shifts in the way you do things as a leader. But these small shifts could add to your organizational, long-term cultural shifts and ultimately bring more effective, creative ideas.

The ten ideas force people to try new things and may make you and your followers feel odd and vulnerable. Yet, vulnerability is a prerequisite for strong creative leadership.[1] For if we don't try new things, experiment, and sometimes fail, surely our followers will not either.

So, have fun with these ideas. Experiment and play, and know that creative leadership sometimes does feel unsettling, a bit odd, and certainly vulnerable.

Ten Small Changes You Can Make to Enhance Creativity in an Organization

Change Your Language

First, leaders can change their language to enhance creativity. Words have power, and leaders need to use that power carefully.

A recent experimental study shows the power of words. In this study, participants made a mistake while writing with a pencil. A number of tools were on their desk, including a rubber band. No eraser was present. When the participants were told, "This is a rubber band," only 3 percent used that rubber band to erase. However, when told "This could be a rubber band," 40 percent realized that it could be used to erase as well.

This experiment begs the question: What limiting language do you unconsciously use that may limit creativity in your organization? Do you categorize work so that certain employees are reluctant to offer input on it? Do you praise a good idea quickly and limit the potential for further ideas to come forth? Or do you negate something without investigating the possible value within that idea?

Changing your language can be an easy way to enhance creativity in your organization. It just takes some thought and care. See Chart 9.1 for ideas.

Chart 9.1 Changing Your Language

From this ...	To this ...
That was a great idea. Let's jump on it.	That's a great idea and may be "the one." But let's take the full week to continue to explore other ideas as well.
That was a good idea, but ...	That was a good idea, and I am interested in talking about how we can make it work within our budget (resources, geography, etc.)
I am not sure that will work.	I wonder how we can make it even more realistic.

Chart 9.1 Changing Your Language (Continued)

From this ...	To this ...
That is against policy.	How can we make that idea work within our policy guidelines?
That seems like it will cost too much.	Let's explore how to make it work on a tight budget. Think outside the box ... we can surely come up with some plan.
It needs more study.	What is next?
We have never done it that way.	I love the originality of the idea.
This is not part of your job/expertise.	That seems like an original idea. I would love to get others input as well ... let's have a meeting with XYZ groups to discuss making it work.

Send Messages that Offer them Immediate Flexibility and Autonomy

Strong transformational leaders give followers freedom at work. Certainly, some projects need to be "managed" and have strict criteria. Yet often, leaders force strict guidelines on all tasks without considering how that control influences the employees' motivation level and opportunity to be creative. Without flexibility and autonomy, followers will complete the project as expected but do little more. Give them flexibility and autonomy, at least on one project, and watch creative ideas emerge.

Tell your followers you want to give them more flexibility and autonomy, and encourage them to take it as an opportunity to develop new ways of thinking and working. Select a project together that you believe they can work on in a more independent way, and then back off. Don't ask questions or hold numerous status meetings. At some point, ask the employee to share progress and setbacks with you. But give it time and space. See Chart 9.2 to guide you.

Chart 9.2 Giving Them Autonomy

From this ...	To this ...
Watching over their every move	Removing yourself from the day-to-day management of the project
Criticize ideas as they come in	Offer feedback on occasion to help them develop new ways of looking at the project

(Continued)

Chart 9.2 Giving Them Autonomy (Continued)

From this ...	To this ...
Daily status meetings with you as the leader	Encourage them to lead their own daily meetings for collaboration purposes
Requiring a set work schedule	Honoring and respecting the schedule they wish to keep, at least in part
Setting a timeline for each of the project's minigoals	Letting others determine the timeline while providing a few "check-in" dates for major milestones
Assign team members	Let the team collaborate as they see useful
Require the team to work together in the office during working hours	Give the team some freedom to work in other locations or venues
Control	Trust

Trying Something New During Your Workday

If you want something new to happen, try something new. Shake things up a bit by trying some of the ideas in Chart 9.3 below.

Chart 9.3 Try Something New

From this ...	To this ...
Meet at the conference room table	Meet on the floor of the conference room, where you have replaced the table with a comfortable rug/blanket
Phone call	Google Hang-Out chat
1-hour status meetings	5-minute "speed" status meetings where participants share short "elevator" speeches with only crucial updates
Meeting in the office	A walking meeting
Catered lunch meeting	Host a "tasting challenge" over lunch: Here, people have to guess the flavor of various items such as chips, soda, or candy. This enhances playfulness among the team and may lead to better relationships
Sit down while working	Work at a counter
Type on your computer	Use voice recognition software to record your unedited ideas about a project
Use black pens	Use colored pens
Listen to your usual radio station while going to work	Turn on an entirely new station
Read your regular newspaper while going to work	Read a new newspaper to gain a fresh perspective

Talk About Your Mistakes

Followers must know that it is safe to make a mistake in your organization. If they fear failure, they will not regularly experiment or try new things. So in order to begin the process of helping followers experiment more, you must vulnerably share your own mistakes with them. Doing so sends a message that failure is accepted and even encouraged in your organization.

Starting today, change the way you talk about failure by using Chart 9.4 below to guide you.

Chart 9.4 Discussing Mistakes

From this ...	To this ...
I understand	I get it. I have made mistakes like that as well
It's okay that you made a mistake	It's okay. Mistakes are part of our work. Let me tell you about the time I really messed up ...
Let's talk about what you did well	Let's talk about what you did well ... (discuss) Great! Let's also talk about whether you are experimenting and risking enough
Be careful	Experiment, take risks!
I did that perfectly	When I started the project, I was terribly unsure how it would go ... it turned out very well though (this shows humility, and that it is okay to be uncertain and imperfect)
I can fix it before anyone finds out	I am going to share my mistake with others so we can learn from it and find the best solution possible
I got this (when unsure about where you are going with a project)	I need help
Let's just move on	Let's see what we can learn from it
I am not going to make any more mistakes	If I don't make any more mistakes, I am not risking enough

Do More than One Project at a Time, but Keep Your Priority in Check

In today's world, we are scattered about in many different directions. Multitasking is becoming our new norm. Yet focusing on one skill makes sense, as it then becomes our priority and has time to blossom. We learn the skill more fully and become an expert in it because our knowledge is vast.

However, it is also helpful to dabble in *something* else, at least occasionally. If you are a scientist, music may spark a new insight for your work. If you study music, it may behoove you to also explore mathematics. This variation in topics, at least from time to time, can add diversity to your experiences, opening you up to new ways of thinking that enhance your overall creativity.

It is also important to consider working on more than one project at a time. For if we focus on only one project, we may push too hard toward completion and miss something along the way. We may avoid real breaks from the project, thereby limiting our opportunities for creativity. And we may miss perspectives on the project that otherwise could come from diversifying our work.

Focusing on a priority makes sense. But focusing on one priority, to the exclusion of all else, is counterproductive for creative leaders. So, let's tweak our lifestyles a bit.

Chart 9.5 Managing Priorities and Time

From this ...	To this ...
Let's put everything we have into this project	Put the project aside from time to time to work on something else
Devote all of your time to work	Pursue an outside interest to help you develop more fully overall and aid in your long-term success as a creative employee
Try hundreds of different types of activities	Try some new activities while also leaving significant time to focus on your expertise and true passions
Tell yourself that diverse interests are wasteful and take effort away from your successes	Tell yourself that opposing interests and activities actually enhance creativity

Change Your Routine

Most of us have daily routines. We wake up, eat the same sorts of foods, take the same route to work, and listen to the same stations. We usually engage with the same people and visit our typical establishments for food, shopping, and entertainment.

Yet, new experiences and perspectives are crucial for creativity. When you visit an entirely new place, you see, smell, and hear new ways of living. Sometimes, these new ways of living create an unexpected connection to your current work or life, thereby enhancing your thinking and lead to new ideas.

Creatives need to break free from routines. And doing so is rather easy. You just need to be purposeful about it, as shown in Chart 9.6 below.

Chart 9.6 Small Shifts in Your Habitual Behaviors

From this ...	To this ...
Stare at social media	Look up tutorials to help you learn something new: perhaps you learn to draw a flower, make an origami bird, or cook a soufflé
Write a standard email	Create an email that rhymes
Play your regular crossword	Try a new brain game like Sudoku, scrabble, or dominoes
Cook your stand-by dinner	Cook an entirely new dish tonight
Let your instrument collect dust	Pick up your instrument for 5 minutes just to play ...
Watch your standard TV show	Watch a video of a symphony, opera, or play
Type your document in the usual way	Change the font and color, just for fun (you can always change it back)
Take notes at a conference	Doodle notes at the conference. See the work of Mark Rhode, Sunni Brown, or Dan Roam to understand the power of doodling
Pray	Pray in color ... when worried about a friend, pray for them by drawing a heart, putting his name inside of it, and asking for help. This is a simple, memorable, and new way to pray, and demonstrates how easy it is to do something different[2]
Shop at your usual grocery store	Shop at an ethnic market
Walk through your department store as usual	Browse a new aisle at the department store
Go to your favorite restaurant	Try a new restaurant
Order your favorite sandwich at lunch	Explore the menu with a keener eye, considering options you don't normally eat
Do your regular routine at the gym	Take a new class, step on a different machine, or try an otherwise unfamiliar approach to your workout

Some of these ideas are profoundly simple and can easily be incorporated into your everyday life. By trying a new routine, you may change your perspective, find greater joy, and open yourself up to new possibilities and ideas. So turn the channel and watch something completely different. Read a genre of books you have never touched or explore a new restaurant and write in purple pen.

Purposefully Infuse Creativity into Your Day and Keep an Idea Journal

If you want to be more creative, you must purposefully work to expand your creativity. I encourage you to take ten minutes of your day to paint, draw, doodle, pick up an instrument, write a poem, or draft a story about your company and its mission.

As well, consider keeping an idea journal, just as Thomas Edison, Leonardo da Vinci, and Benjamin Franklin did. Your task is to create an electronic or written journal that can be easily accessed. Then, as you go about your day, write down, draw, or record anything that is of interest to you in this journal. Are you drawn to a quote today, or a particular article? Save it in your journal, even if it may not be completely relevant to your current reality. Then, every few months, look back at your journal and notice whether any of the information can be used in a relevant way to help solve problems in the workplace.

By infusing creativity into your day through writing, art, music and/ or idea journals, you will grow as a creative individual and begin to model that for your followers. Over time, you will find that these small purposeful acts enhanced your life and leadership and were quite easy to do. Remember that it is important to not judge the outcome here. The goal is simply to enjoy being a bit more creative, in a purposeful way, for a few minutes each day. Chart 9.7 outlines a few ideas to get you started.

Chart 9.7 Daily Creative Spurts

From this ...	To this ...
Review your company's mission	Draft a story about your company and its mission
Browse social media	Draw a picture or doodling

Chart 9.7 Daily Creative Spurts (Continued)

From this ...	To this ...
Exercise for an hour	Exercise harder for 45 minutes and take 10 minutes to pick up an instrument
Look at recipes on Pinterest	Create a new meal for dinner tonight by experimentation (vs. following a recipe)
Listen to music	Try to create a mash up of the last two songs you heard on the radio
Print an article to reference later	Save the article in your idea journal
Jot down a quote on a scrap piece of paper	Save the quote in your idea journal

Brainstorm in a New Way

We all brainstorm solutions at some point in our lives. Perhaps we create a list of options individually or do so in large group meetings. Often, the list-making is done in an informal way, with people sharing ideas randomly at a table. This can be useful. However, there are a number of simple tools that can be used to enhance creativity in brainstorming sessions.

First, try to break out of your routine with brainstorming. If you always do it alone, try to brainstorm with others. If you brainstorm only with others, consider trying it on your own.

If you always begin brainstorming in a group verbally, consider trying a new method. Perhaps you begin by asking each participant to write down their own ideas, with verbal sharing done following this personal reflection time. You could also brainstorm in writing, without speaking a word. Here, each person could draft two to three ideas on paper. Then, they rotate the paper to the person next to them. On this new piece of paper, each person must add two new ideas. The papers should rotate several times, generating a long list of options when all compiled together.

Changing your method for brainstorming does not usually take additional time but can quickly enhance the creativity and engagement in a room. Adding a written component may generate ideas from introverted employees. Incubation time may help bring new ideas to the table when you split an hour session into five short sessions dispersed throughout the week. Below are a few more ideas to help you brainstorm in a new way.

Chart 9.8 New Methods for Developing Ideas

From this ...	To this ...
Individual brainstorming	Brainstorm with a friend/colleague
Brainstorm with a group	Try it alone first
Brainstorm at a desk	Brainstorm outside
Brainstorm for 10 minutes	Brainstorm for an hour
Brainstorm in 1 session	Brainstorm in several small sessions spread throughout the week
Brainstorm verbally	Brainstorm in writing
Brainstorm in words	Brainstorm in pictures
Brainstorm while sitting	Brainstorm while standing or lying on the ground
Brainstorm in a meeting	Informally brainstorm over a meal
Brainstorm with your team	Bring in an outsider(s) who knows nothing about the problem to brainstorm solutions
Brainstorm using words alone	When brainstorming, use a corresponding gesture or movement with each shared idea.

The ideas listed above may enhance the playfulness of the brainstorming session or bring in a fresh perspective. Adding visuals or movement to the session adds to the spirit of play and also solidifies concepts for the visual or kinesthetic learner. Having a session outside or simply lying down brings unique perspectives and may enhance originality.

In addition, there are several popular brainstorming methods that can be purposefully interjected into your meetings and work to enhance creativity in quick bursts. SCAMPER is one of the more commonly used methods.

SCAMPER is a brainstorming tool, created by Bob Eberle, that helps generate new ideas.[3] It is a mnemonic, containing a collection of techniques to help people think differently when they become stuck while problem solving. The SCAMPER method encourages people to force a response, no matter how ridiculous. In order to use SCAMPER, participants should apply the following ideas to their problem:

S—Substitute: Here, you remove some part of the accepted situation or concept and replace it with something else.

For example, if you were working on a new marketing campaign for a coaching company, you would remove print as a medium. Fliers, invitations, and letters no longer exist. How could you effectively market? Develop a full list of ideas, with that premise in mind.

C—Combine: Here, you join or force together two or more elements and consider how such a combination might move you toward a solution.

Returning to the marketing problem, here we need to join two elements together to move forward. You could join together marketing and legal, or marketing and food service to help create new ways to market. If marketing and legal are joined, people may develop an idea that involves a "mock trial" where attorneys prove that coaching is a worthwhile investment. If marketing and food service are joined, people may develop ideas to market by sending cupcakes with business cards, or hosting a dinner with speed coaching sessions.

Sometimes, the combinations work and bring forth new and useful ideas. Sometimes, they don't. The trick is to try to develop a list of unique ideas, postponing the evaluation until a later time.

A—Adapt: Here, you change some part of your problem so that it works where it did not before.

For the marketing problem, you could change it to a problem of reach. For instance, it is not about how you market to new people, but rather a problem related to effectively marketing to and reaching your current client base.

M—Modify: Here, you change some of the attributes of the problem. You can do so arbitrarily, if necessary, which may include changing the size, shape, texture, color, history, and so on of the problem.

For marketing, you could consider brainstorming options if this were 1920 or even 2025. How might your materials be different? If it were the 20s, you would make house calls and send handwritten letters. If it were 2025, maybe you will be sending packages by drones or developing a campaign where people pay what they deem fair for the services. Another way to modify would be to change the size of the materials. Perhaps you want to develop small marketing materials such as a 2-inch book about your services or a minifigurine representing your company.

Again, you don't need perfect answers. You just need to **M**odify the attributes to come up with different ideas to expand your thinking and creativity.

P—Purpose (Put to other use): Here, you modify the intention of the subject, challenging why it exists and what it is supposed to do. Your goal is to challenge these assumptions and suggest new and unusual purposes.

People use marketing to gain new clients. They want more money and success, and market to enhance that. With the **Purpose** exercise, we explore this concept more deeply, asking why the coaches need to market at all? Maybe they should just improve their work and expect referrals.

E—Eliminate: Here, you remove any or all elements of your subject in order to simplify and reduce it to the core function.

With marketing, your core function is to attract more clients. Keeping that in mind, remove some part of marketing as an option when brainstorming. For instance, when you remove paper marketing as a possibility, you know you can market through blogs, emails, and social media. When you remove social media and blogs as well, you can market through conferences, speaking engagements, and affiliation arrangements.

R—Reverse and/or Rearrange: Here you change orientation, turning things upside down or inside out, against the direction it was intended to go or be used.

In our coaching example, you could ask your clients to market and sell their services to you, rather than you marketing to them. Doing so may provide you with new insight into their work and help you discover original ways to serve them. As well, you could create an event whereby your clients market and network with each other.

As you can see, the **SCAMPER** technique is a simple way to make brainstorming more productive, engaging, and creative. It brings new, fresh insight and sparks creativity as well. It is easy to implement all of the components, or just one, into your next idea session or work meeting.

Choose One New Person to Work with this Week

We want to collaborate more. It encourages creativity, helps bring new ideas to the table, and enhances success. So, pull one new person onto a project this week. Consider pulling in someone from a different department, or a person from a different culture or generation. Explore their point of view with great curiosity and ask them how they might solve a problem. Chart 9.9 below provides additional ideas.

Chart 9.9 Diversify Your Teams

From this ...	To this ...
Work with the same partner	Pull in the new intern to give you ideas on the project
Work with the new employee	Bring in the most seasoned employee to give you perspective on the project
Work independently	Ask a group to offer feedback on the project, even if only for an hour
Work within your department	Call on people from a different department to offer feedback
Stay within your office to get feedback	Ask your friend in a different industry for her perspective
Thank someone for feedback on your work	Thank them, but also ask who else might be able to offer unique ideas
Talk sports at lunch with your coworkers	Ask your co-workers to share details about their projects while offering your own "outsider's perspective" on the work

Then, encourage followers to tweak their conversations and collaborations in a similar way.

Let Time Be Your Ally

The creative process requires pauses and incubation. Yet we live in a culture of "busyness" and action. In these moments, it is difficult to be your best self. For rarely do we feel connection and creativity while urgently drafting documents, responding to emails, or running into and out of meetings.

Thus, in order to enhance our creativity, we must mindfully pause and encourage our followers to do the same. These pauses may bring reflection, sparks of inspiration, and a feeling of centered authenticity. Consider adopting some of the ideas in Chart 9.10 in next page.

Chart 9.10 Reflect and Take Your Time

From this ...	To this ...
Scan social media	Look out the window
Listen to the radio while driving to work	Drive in silence
Eat while watching television	Eat quietly, with no agenda
Work through lunch	Take a short walk during lunch
Respond immediately to emails and messages	Set aside hands-free time to reflect and pause
Turn on a movie or show at night	Listen to music with your eyes closed
Run with headphones	Run in silence
Rush to clear the plates after dinner	Sit for some extra time to enjoy your family and/or the quiet
Check emails and other items right before bed	Meditate, pray, or just sit in silence right before bed
End a brainstorming session early because everyone has gone silent	Continue the session, even if there is silence, because you know silence is sometimes needed to produce great ideas
Move to action items when a great idea is presented at work	Take more time to develop and think about great ideas, rather than jump on the first good one
Write your to-do list quickly	Thoughtfully write a list of truly important work you want to accomplish

Taking your time in a thoughtful way will enhance your leadership and creativity. You will be more reflective, wise, and authentic, and leave room for creativity to blossom. As well, by pausing, you give others a chance to shine, which is important to your organization's success.

Conclusion

Leadership is an ongoing, evolving process. As a strong leader, you will need to make leadership and cultural changes in order to enhance creativity. You will work to become transformational and seek opportunities for collaboration, effective training, and creative spaces. You will work with intention, purpose, and determination in order to support your employees and their new ideas. And you will become more creative yourself, respecting the creative process, honoring playfulness and experimentation, and making mistakes every now and again.

Leading in this way is hard work. It is risky. Yet, with consistent attention, you will find your employees are not only more creative, they are also happier, more engaged, and more effective. And you are as well.

It won't be easy. But it will be worth it.

Reflection Questions

1. What small change can I make in my language to encourage creativity today?
2. How can I break out of routine, at least a little bit, today?
3. How can I make today's work a bit different? Should we take a walk during our meeting? Should I work for an hour with only a pen and paper?
4. What would I really love to do creatively? Paint, write, play an instrument? What can I put down in order to make time for my creative interests?
5. When can I run a brainstorming session using SCAMPER as a guide?
6. Where can I build in 10 minutes to sit and "do nothing?"
7. What project can I step away from a little this week in order to give employees more autonomy? When can I tell my employees "I trust you, and want you to run with the project as you see fit?"
8. What mistake can I share with others? When will I share?

Notes

1. For more on vulnerability, see Brene Brown's work, including Brown, Brené. *Daring Greatly: How the Courage to Be Vulnerable Transforms the Way We Live, Love, Parent, and Lead.* New York, NY: Gotham Books, 2012.
2. For more on this concept, see MacBeth, Sybil. *Praying in Color: Drawing a New Path to God.* Brewster, MA: Paraclete Press, 2007.
3. Eberle, B. (2008). Scamper: Let Your Imagination Run Wild. For more ideas, see www.mindtools.com/pages/article/newCT_02.htm

Index

OTHER TITLES IN THE HUMAN RESOURCE MANAGEMENT AND ORGANIZATIONAL BEHAVIOR COLLECTION

- *Fostering Creativity in Self and the Organization: Your Professional Edge* by Eric W. Stein
- *Designing Creative High Power Teams and Organization: Beyond Leadership* by Eric W. Stein
- *Creating a Pathway to Your Dream Career: Designing and Controlling a Career Around Your Life Goals* by Tom Kucharvy
- *Leader Evolution: From Technical Expertise to Strategic Leadership* by Alan Patterson
- *Followership: What It Takes to Lead* by James H. Schindler
- *The Search For Best Practices: Doing the Right Thing the Right Way* by Rob Reider
- *Marketing Your Value: 9 Steps to Navigate Your Career* by Michael Edmondson
- *Competencies at Work: Providing a Common Language for Talent Management* by Enrique Washington and Bruce Griffiths
- *Manage Your Career: 10 Keys to Survival and Success When Interviewing and on the Job, Second Edition* by Vijay Sathe
- *You're A Genius: Using Reflective Practice to Master the Craft of Leadership* by Steven S. Taylor
- *Major in Happiness: Debunking the College Major Fallacies* by Michael Edmondson
- *The Resilience Advantage: Stop Managing Stress and Find Your Resilience* by Richard S. Citrin and Alan Weiss
- *Success: Theory and Practice* by Michael Edmondson
- *Leading The Positive Organization: Actions, Tools, and Processes* by Thomas N. Duening

Announcing the Business Expert Press Digital Library

Concise e-books business students need for classroom and research

This book can also be purchased in an e-book collection by your library as

- a one-time purchase,
- that is owned forever,
- allows for simultaneous readers,
- has no restrictions on printing, and
- can be downloaded as PDFs from within the library community.

Our digital library collections are a great solution to beat the rising cost of textbooks. E-books can be loaded into their course management systems or onto student's e-book readers.

The **Business Expert Press** digital libraries are very affordable, with no obligation to buy in future years. For more information, please visit **www.businessexpertpress.com/librarians**. To set up a trial in the United States, please contact **sales@businessexpertpress.com**.